Hands United

The Collective Journey
Towards a Kinder World

by
ASHLEY KINSTONA

This book is dedicated to all who practice charity in one form or another, big and small. Your actions have made lives better and the world a better place

Contents

Introduction

In a world teeming with challenges and hardships, the light of charity shines as a beacon of hope and solidarity. The act of giving, in its many forms, holds the power to transform lives, communities, and eventually, the very fabric of society. This book is devoted to unraveling the essence of charity, illuminating its core and expounding on the profound need for every individual to extend a helping hand whenever possible.

At its heart, charity is an expression of empathy and compassion, a testament to the human capacity for kindness. It's a concept that stretches across borders, cultures, and religions, uniting people under the common goal of alleviating suffering and making the world a slightly better place. Yet, despite its universal appeal, the nuances of charity and the most effective ways to contribute are often misunderstood.

This introduction serves as a gateway to the broader conversation about charity. It aims to inspire, inform, and ignite a passion for giving. Through the exploration of what charity truly means, we embark on a journey that goes beyond mere financial donations, delving into the multitude of ways one can make a difference. It's about recognizing need, understanding the impact of our actions, and fostering a culture of generosity that spans generations.

If the idea of charity conjures images of grandiose gestures and hefty cheques, it's time to expand that vision. True charity is embedded in the everyday acts of kindness—sharing a smile, lending a listening ear, or offering a word of encouragement. These simple acts of compassion are the building blocks of a more charitable world.

The need for a helping hand has never been greater. In an era marked by significant social, economic, and environmental challenges, the call to action is loud and clear. Yet, the problem many face isn't apathy but a lack of understanding of where to start. This book aims to bridge that gap, equipping readers with the knowledge and motivation to take that crucial first step.

Exploring the essence of charity will uncover the deep roots this ancient practice has in human history and its evolution over time. The journey will reveal charity's role in modern society, transcending religious obligations and becoming a universal value that promotes psychological well-being, fosters community, and drives global change.

Each chapter of this book has been carefully crafted to cover a specific facet of charity. From personal stories of hope and help to the impact of technology on charitable giving, the narrative weaves together a comprehensive picture that highlights both the beauty and complexities of being charitable.

Moreover, this book confronts the challenges faced by philanthropic efforts. It scrutinizes the oft-overlooked dark side of charity, including the misuse of funds and the potential for harm. By addressing these issues head-on, it aims to guide readers toward more sustainable, respectful, and impactful forms of giving.

Charity is not a one-way street; it's a path of mutual growth and enlightenment. The psychological benefits of giving, for both the giver and the receiver, are profound. This book delves into how helping others does indeed help us, fostering a sense of joy, purpose, and connection in our lives.

Furthermore, charity begins at home. Fostering a culture of generosity within families plants the seeds for lifelong values of empathy, kindness, and social responsibility. This book offers insights into teaching children about charity, thus ensuring that the ripple effect of kindness continues to spread far and wide.

Technology has opened up new frontiers for charity, changing the ways we give and engage with causes. From the rise of crowdfunding to the role of social media in advocacy and activism, this book explores the opportunities and challenges presented by the digital revolution in philanthropy.

In a world often marked by divisions, charity stands as a unifying force. By participating in charitable endeavors, we not only address immediate needs but also contribute to building a more just, compassionate, and sustainable world. This book invites readers to become part of this transformative movement, to be not just bystanders but active participants in the story of charity.

The future of charity is an exciting and evolving narrative, with innovations in giving and new approaches to volunteerism and philanthropy emerging. This book looks ahead, considering how we can all contribute to a culture of kindness and ensure that the spirit of charity thrives for generations to come.

In closing, this introduction is but the first step on a fascinating journey. It's an invitation to see the world through the lens of compassion, to recognize our shared humanity, and to act on the compelling urge to make a difference. With each page turned, may this book inspire a renewed commitment to charity, in all its forms, and motivate us to offer a helping hand whenever and wherever it's needed.

Let us embark on this journey together, exploring the many faces of charity, navigating its challenges, and celebrating its triumphs. For in the act of giving, we find true meaning, purpose, and connection— qualities that enrich not only the lives of those we help but our own as well.

Chapter 1:
The Essence of Charity

At the heart of every compassionate act, lies the essence of charity: a profound understanding that we are all connected, each of us a thread in the fabric of humanity. Charity isn't just about the simple act of giving—it's a testament to our collective spirit and a cornerstone of human kindness. This fundamental principle guides us through the complexities of altruism, urging us to look beyond our individual desires and consider the greater good. With every act of charity, we're not just offering a helping hand; we're affirming our role in a larger community, recognizing that the well-being of others directly influences our own. As we embark on this journey to delve deeper into the significance of giving, let's keep in mind that charity is more than an external expression of compassion—it's a mirror reflecting our most innate human values. Armed with the knowledge and motivation to make a difference, we begin to unveil the true power of charity, which, at its core, is love in action. Through understanding our role, exploring historical perspectives, and observing charity in modern society, we will unearth the layers that compose the heart of charitable endeavors, setting the stage for a transformative exploration of generosity's boundless potential.

Understanding Our Role

In the vast tapestry of human connection, charity emerges as a compelling thread, weaving stories of compassion, resilience, and transformation. Each of us, regardless of our background or beliefs, carries the potential to leave an indelible mark on this narrative through acts of kindness and generosity. Recognizing our role within this context doesn't just involve understanding the mechanics of giving, but also appreciating the profound impact our contributions can have on the lives of others and on society as a whole. It's about seeing beyond our immediate circle and acknowledging that our actions—no matter how small they might seem—can ripple through communities, forging bonds of solidarity and hope. This section isn't just a call to action; it's an invitation to embark on a journey of self-discovery and purpose, to explore the depths of what it means to truly give, and to recognize that in the act of helping others, we often find ourselves enriched in ways we never anticipated. As we dive into the historical and modern perspectives of charity in the subsequent sections, remember that our collective endeavor to make the world a better place starts with each individual decision to extend a hand, to listen, and to care.

The Historical Perspective on charity unveils a story woven through the fabric of human society, echoing the intrinsic desire to aid those in need. This tale, as ancient as humanity itself, reveals manifestations of benevolence that have shaped civilizations and their core values.

Tracing back to the earliest civilizations, the acts of giving and assistance were not merely transactions but were imbued with moral and spiritual significance. Ancient texts and edicts, from the Code of Hammurabi to the teachings within the Vedas, the Bible, and the Quran, all highlight charity as a virtue indispensable to the welfare of society. This underscores a universal acknowledgment across diverse cultures and religions that to give is to sustain the very essence of community life.

In the shadows of great empires and spiritual movements, charity evolved. It became more structured with the establishment of almshouses and hospitals in medieval Europe, showcasing a transition from individual acts of charity to institutionalized assistance. These foundations were the precursors to modern social services, born out of a collective responsibility towards the less fortunate.

The Renaissance period rekindled the importance of personal virtue in charitable acts, emphasizing benevolence as a reflection of one's character. This era witnessed the emergence of philanthropy intertwined with the arts and education, signifying a broadening perspective on what it means to contribute to society's welfare beyond mere survival.

Fast forward to the Industrial Revolution, and the landscape of charity underwent yet another transformation. As societies grappled with unprecedented social and economic changes, philanthropists like Andrew Carnegie and John D. Rockefeller harnessed their wealth to address the burgeoning needs of the time. Their contributions laid the groundwork for modern philanthropic endeavors, blending charity with strategic approaches to solving societal issues.

The 20th century further diversified charity through the advent of non-profit organizations and NGOs, reflecting a globalization of compassion. These entities tackled global challenges, from hunger and health to education and equality, signaling a shift from local acts of kindness to a collective global effort.

However, the ethos of charity remained consistent; it's an expression of the shared human experience, a testament to our interconnectedness. Acts of charity, no matter the scale or form, speak to a fundamental aspect of what it means to be human: to empathize, to support, and to uplift.

Yet, understanding charity solely through a historical lens would be an incomplete picture without recognizing the personal stories intertwined with these acts. Each act of charity carries with it a narrative of hope, resilience, and a desire for a more equitable world. These stories, often unrecorded in the annals of history, are what truly animate the spirit of charity.

In many ways, the history of charity is a mirror reflecting societal norms, values, and the underlying challenges of eras. It also serves as a beacon, guiding future generations on the path of empathy and action. This historical tapestry does not just recount acts of giving but underscores the evolving nature of human compassion and its capacity to transform societies.

Indeed, as we stand on the shoulders of those who came before us, it becomes clear that charity is not merely about the transfer of resources but about bridging divides. It's about recognizing the dignity in every individual and acting upon the inherent desire to make a difference in their lives.

Thus, the historical perspective on charity offers a compelling narrative, one that intertwines with the fabric of humanity itself. It serves as a reminder that at every pivotal moment in history, there have been individuals and communities willing to extend a helping hand, to offer solace, to inspire change. This narrative is not just about the past; it's a call to action for the present and the future.

The essence of charity, nurtured over millennia, highlights an immutable truth: that to give is part of our collective identity. It transcends time, cultures, and societal changes, solidifying its place as a cornerstone of human civilization. This historical journey of charity, fraught with challenges and triumphs, exemplifies the resilience and generosity innate in humanity.

It's in reflecting on this journey that we find the motivation to continue the legacy of giving. The historical perspective on charity doesn't just teach us about where we have been; it inspires us where we need to go. It beckons us to carry forward the torch of compassion, to illuminate the dark corners of inequality and suffering with acts of kindness that have the power to change the world.

In sum, the historical perspective on charity is a sweeping saga of human solidarity. It's a story that reminds us that in every act of giving, no matter how small, lies the potential to write a new chapter in the ongoing narrative of humanity's quest for a better world. As we forge ahead, let this perspective galvanize us to act with courage, to give with purpose, and to believe in the transformative power of charity.

Thus, as we continue to navigate the complexities of modern society, let us draw strength from the historical roots of charity. Let it remind us that at the heart of every civilization, past, present, and future, lies the noble act of helping one another. It is this enduring spirit of generosity that has the power to unite us, inspire change, and foster a culture of kindness that transcends all barriers.

Charity in Modern Society The world we live in has evolved in countless ways, from the advent of digital communication to the globalization of economies. Amidst these sweeping changes, the concept of charity has also found new avenues for expression and challenges that necessitate a modern understanding.

In today's society, charity goes beyond the mere act of giving to encompass a broader spectrum of actions aimed at uplifting and supporting those in need. It's about creating a ripple of positive change that can traverse communities, borders, and continents. The essence of being charitable has expanded; it's no longer confined to the wealthy donating to the poor but includes everyday acts of kindness, volunteering time, and sharing resources.

One of the most significant shifts has been the democratization of giving, facilitated by technology. Online platforms make it possible for anyone with internet access to donate to causes they care about with a click of a button. Crowdfunding campaigns can rally thousands of small contributions to achieve substantial impacts, from covering medical bills to supporting disaster relief efforts.

Despite this ease of access, the digital age presents its own set of challenges. The vast sea of information can sometimes make it difficult to discern the legitimacy of charitable organizations. This underscores the importance of due diligence and informed giving, ensuring that one's contributions genuinely help those in need.

Moreover, the visibility of charity has increased. Social media allows for acts of kindness to be shared and celebrated across platforms, inspiring others to take action. While this visibility can certainly amplify the effects of charity, it also raises questions about the motivations behind charitable acts. In a world where everything is shared, the line between altruism and the desire for social recognition can become blurred.

Corporate social responsibility (CSR) has also taken center stage, with businesses recognizing their role in societal welfare. Companies large and small are integrating charity into their business models, whether through donating a portion of profits, supporting employee volunteering, or engaging in partnerships with nonprofit organizations. This shift not only benefits communities but also builds a more compassionate corporate culture.

Global challenges, such as climate change, poverty, and inequality, require collaborative solutions. Modern charity is increasingly about building networks of support that can tackle these issues on multiple fronts. It's about leveraging resources, knowledge, and innovation to create sustainable change.

Despite the expanded avenues for charitable giving, the heart of charity remains the same: empathy. The ability to understand and share the feelings of another person is a timeless driver of charitable acts. Today, empathy also means recognizing the interconnectedness of our world and understanding that helping others, near or far, ultimately benefits us all.

Engaging in modern charity also demands a critical approach. It involves asking questions about the impact of one's contributions and seeking out ways to make a difference that go beyond traditional monetary donations. It's about empowering communities rather than creating dependency, ensuring that aid provides a pathway to self-sufficiency.

Education plays a crucial role in fostering a charitable spirit in modern society. By teaching younger generations about the importance of giving back, we plant the seeds for a more generous future. Moreover, instilling a sense of global citizenship can encourage young people to think broadly about how they can contribute to solving world issues.

Volunteerism has risen as a cornerstone of modern charity. Giving one's time and skills often provides direct, hands-on support that money cannot buy. From teaching and mentoring to environmental conservation efforts, volunteers are the backbone of many charitable initiatives.

Yet, as we navigate the complexities of modern charity, it's essential to hold onto its essence: the genuine desire to help. In a world that's constantly changing, our empathy and compassion are the anchors that keep the spirit of charity strong and vibrant.

As we face a future marked by uncertainty, the importance of charity in modern society cannot be overstated. With each act of kindness, we weave a fabric of support that can hold communities together through difficult times. Charity, in its many forms, is a testament to the enduring human capacity for empathy and generosity.

Ultimately, the evolution of charity reflects the evolution of society itself. As we push the boundaries of what it means to give, we also redefine what it means to be part of a global community. In this era of unprecedented change, charity remains a universal value that can unite us in our common humanity and drive us towards a brighter, more compassionate future.

So let's embrace the opportunities and challenges of charity in modern society. By understanding its nuances and adapting our approach, we can all play a part in creating a world where generosity and kindness are woven into the fabric of everyday life. The act of giving, in all its forms, is more than a moral duty; it's a testament to our shared humanity and a beacon of hope for future generations.

Chapter 2:
Beyond Religion: Charity as a Universal Value

As we transition from exploring the rich tapestry of charity's essence, it's pivotal to recognize that the act of giving transcends the boundaries of religious teachings and doctrines. While numerous faiths prescribe charity as a fundamental practice, the impulse to lend a helping hand is a universal value that resides in the heart of humanity itself. This chapter delves into how charity operates beyond the realms of religion, asserting itself as a universal ethos that unites us all.

At its core, charity is about extending kindness to others without expecting anything in return. This principle is not exclusive to any one faith; rather, it is a golden thread weaving through the fabric of human society. Across cultures and civilizations, offering support to those in need has been a cornerstone of moral conduct and communal harmony.

History is replete with tales of altruism that know no religious bounds. From ancient civilizations to modern societies, the act of giving has always been a beacon of hope and a testament to the strength of the human spirit. Charity, in its purest form, is the embodiment of empathy and compassion—qualities inherent to all human beings, regardless of their spiritual beliefs.

The notion that we are all part of a larger community is a powerful motivator for charitable acts. It compels individuals to look beyond their immediate surroundings and consider the well-being of others.

This sense of interconnectedness fosters a culture of giving that benefits society as a whole, paving the way for a more cohesive and compassionate world.

Moreover, the value of charity is increasingly recognized in secular contexts as well. Governments, corporations, and individuals alike are beginning to see the importance of philanthropy in addressing societal challenges. From combating poverty to improving education, charity serves as a versatile tool for social transformation.

It's essential to understand that charity is not merely about financial donations. Acts of service, such as volunteering time or sharing skills, embody the spirit of charity just as much. These contributions, though intangible, have the potential to make a profound impact on the lives of others.

The universality of charity is a reminder that our capacity for kindness is not limited to certain times, places, or beliefs. Every act of generosity, big or small, contributes to a larger narrative of compassion that transcends cultural and religious divides.

Embracing charity as a universal value also challenges us to rethink our approach to giving. It encourages us to adopt a more inclusive perspective, one that respects and values the diversity of ways in which people choose to contribute to the betterment of society.

This recognition of charity's broad scope invites us to explore new avenues for collaboration and innovation. By pooling resources and knowledge, we can tackle complex social issues more effectively, drawing on the strengths of various traditions and practices.

Furthermore, the universal appeal of charity has the power to inspire a sense of responsibility in each of us. It nudges us to consider our role in the world and how we can make a positive difference. This reflection is crucial for cultivating a culture of generosity that will endure for generations to come.

As we move forward, it's vital to foster dialogue and exchange among different communities about the meaning and practice of charity. Sharing insights and experiences can enrich our understanding and inspire more people to embrace the art of giving.

In essence, charity as a universal value offers a vision of a united humanity, working hand in hand towards a common goal of alleviating suffering and enhancing the quality of life for all. This vision compels us to act with kindness, extending our support to those in need, regardless of the invisible lines that might otherwise divide us.

At its heart, charity challenges us to be our best selves, to reach out with open hands and hearts. In doing so, we not only help others but also discover the true richness of the human spirit—a richness that flourishes in the acts of giving and receiving in kind.

In conclusion, while the practice of charity may originate from religious teachings for many, its essence and impact go far beyond. Charity is a testament to what can be achieved when compassion, empathy, and generosity guide our actions. By embracing charity as a universal value, we can forge a path towards a more inclusive, caring, and harmonious world.

As we advance to the subsequent chapters, let's carry forward the understanding that charity, in its myriad forms, is a profound expression of our shared humanity. It's an invitation to step beyond our differences and unite in the common cause of supporting and uplifting one another. In this spirit, may we continue to explore the depth and breadth of charity and its capacity to transform both giver and receiver alike.

Chapter 3:
The Psychological Benefits of Being Charitable

Diving into the heart of charity, we uncover a profound truth: the act of giving not only transforms the lives of recipients but also enriches the soul of the giver. The psychological benefits of being charitable are vast and deeply impactful, creating ripples of joy and fulfillment that reach far beyond the immediate act of giving. When we extend a helping hand, we're not just offering financial support or material goods; we're also fostering a sense of connection, empathy, and shared humanity. This act of kindness triggers a cascade of positive emotions within us—happiness, gratitude, and a deep sense of satisfaction that comes from knowing we've made a tangible difference in someone's life.

Moreover, being charitable nurtures our mental health, acting as a buffer against the harsh winds of stress, depression, and loneliness that often plague modern existence. It's a reminder that we're part of something larger than ourselves, a community where each gesture of kindness strengthens the bonds that tie us together. This chapter explores how altruism enriches our lives, touching on the psychological rewards that accompany generous behavior. Amidst the complexities of life, the simplicity of giving emerges as a beacon of hope and happiness, illuminating the path to a more fulfilled and compassionate existence.

The Joy of Giving

At the heart of the human experience lies a simple, yet profound truth: giving enriches us in ways material wealth never can. Embarking on the journey of charity, we discover the indescribable joy that comes from lending a hand to someone in need. This act of giving, far from depleting our resources, fills us with an unmatched sense of fulfillment and purpose. It's a paradox that the more we give, the richer we become – not in our bank accounts, but in our souls. Science backs this up, showing that acts of kindness are linked to increased feelings of well-being. Whether it's sharing time, resources, or simply a kind word, each effort reverberates through our lives, teaching us empathy and reinforcing the deep-seated connection we share with those around us. Through the act of giving, we step outside ourselves and participate in something larger, something inherently beautiful. This chapter isn't just about understanding the mechanics of charity; it's an invitation to bask in the joy of giving and to let that joy transform us.

How Helping Others Helps Us As we journey through the essence of charity, it's time to turn our gaze inwards and look at the other side of the equation. Why do we, as individuals, choose to extend a helping hand? What compels us to offer support beyond our own needs and desires? It's not merely about fulfilling a societal or moral obligation; there's more to it, deeply ingrained within our psyche. This exploration is not just about understanding the altruistic side of human nature but also about uncovering the reciprocal benefits that charity bestows upon the giver.

The act of helping others, whether through time, resources, or emotional support, triggers an intrinsic reward system in our brains. Pioneering studies have shown that charitable activities light up the same regions associated with pleasure and reward. This isn't just psychological jargon but a real, tangible feeling of happiness and satisfaction that emanates from the act of giving. It's as if our brains are hardwired to feel good when we do good. This serotonin boost can lead to what's popularly known as the 'helper's high,' a state of euphoria or deep satisfaction after helping others.

On a deeper level, engaging in charitable activities fosters a sense of connection and belonging. Our society, despite its advancements, often feels fragmented and isolated. Helping others acts as a bridge, reducing feelings of loneliness and creating a sense of community. This isn't something abstract but a fact rooted in our biological need for social interaction. Humans are social creatures, and charity offers a pathway to meet this intrinsic need, filling our lives with meaningful relationships and a sense of being part of something bigger than ourselves.

Beyond the psychological and emotional benefits, there's a significant impact on our physical health when we engage in acts of charity. Research has revealed that individuals who volunteer regularly have lower blood pressure, reduced stress levels, and a longer lifespan. It's as if altruism not only enriches our souls but also heals our bodies. This connection between physical health and charity underscores the holistic benefit of helping others, serving as a powerful reminder of how intertwined our well-being is with the act of giving.

Engaging in acts of kindness and generosity also enhances our sense of purpose and identity. In a world fraught with existential questions and quests for meaning, charity offers a straightforward answer. It provides us with a sense of direction and fulfillment, grounding our lives in values that extend beyond material success or personal achievements. This isn't to say that charity is the sole answer to life's questions but it's a vital piece of the puzzle that adds depth and richness to our existence.

Moreover, being charitable cultivates empathy and compassion within us. It pushes us to consider the perspectives, suffering, and needs of others, expanding our emotional repertoire and making us more understanding and kind individuals. This isn't just beneficial for those we help; it's a profound personal growth experience that enhances our emotional intelligence, making us better listeners, friends, partners, and citizens.

Charity also offers an opportunity for skill development and learning. Whether it's organizing a local food drive, mentoring youth, or contributing to a global fundraising campaign, these activities challenge us to use and improve our abilities. This isn't just about adding a line on a resume but about real, applicable skills that can enhance our personal and professional lives. The lessons learned through charity are often those that can't be taught in a traditional setting, fostering creativity, leadership, and problem-solving abilities.

Participating in charitable endeavors can also lead to a change in perspective, shifting our focus from what we lack to what we have. This gratitude mindset is a powerful antidote to the incessant desire for more that plagues modern society. By helping others, we're reminded of our own blessings, fostering a sense of contentment and appreciation for the simple things in life. This shift in focus is profound, moving us towards a more fulfilling and joyful existence.

The benefits of helping others extend even to overcoming personal challenges and struggles. For some, charity offers a path out of the darkness, a way to channel personal pain into something positive. It's not uncommon to hear stories of individuals who, in the process of helping others, find healing for themselves. Whether it's battling addiction, coping with loss, or overcoming depression, charity provides a constructive outlet for our trials, transforming our struggles into sources of strength.

Furthermore, engaging in charity can enhance our social skills and deepen our relationships. It offers common ground with like-minded individuals, fostering friendships and connections that are rooted in shared values and goals. These aren't just superficial ties but meaningful relationships that can offer support, inspiration, and companionship on our journey through life. The social aspect of charity is often overlooked, but it's a critical component of the reciprocal benefits of helping others.

In a world that often emphasizes individual achievement and success, charity offers a counter-narrative. It shifts the measure of a life well-lived from what we acquire to what we give. This isn't a call to abandon personal goals but to integrate acts of kindness and generosity into our definition of success. The fulfillment that comes from helping others adds a layer of meaning to our achievements, enriching our lives beyond the material.

Moreover, the act of helping others can act as a powerful tool for breaking down barriers and prejudices. Through charity, we encounter individuals and communities we might never engage with otherwise. These experiences challenge our preconceptions and biases, fostering a more inclusive and empathetic worldview. This isn't just theoretical; it's a practical pathway to a more harmonious and understanding society.

On a philosophical level, engaging in charity connects us with a tradition of altruism that spans cultures and history. It's a way of participating in a legacy of kindness that transcends personal and temporal boundaries. This connection to a larger narrative of human compassion adds a layer of profundity to our charitable acts, reminding us that we're part of a long lineage of individuals who have sought to make the world a better place.

In the journey toward self-improvement and personal growth, charity plays a pivotal role. It offers a unique combination of joy, fulfillment, and perspective that challenges and enriches us. This isn't to say that the path of charity is always easy or straightforward. It requires sacrifice, empathy, and a willingness to step out of our comfort zones. However, the rewards, both for those we help and for ourselves, are immense. In the final analysis, the act of helping others does indeed help us, filling our lives with meaning, joy, and a deep sense of connection to the world around us.

As we reflect on the multitude of ways in which charity benefits us, let us also remember the primary goal: to make a difference in the lives of others. This doesn't invalidate the personal gains we've explored but places them in the broader context of altruism's true essence. It's a beautiful cycle of giving and receiving, where the line between helper and helped blurs, and we find ourselves united in the shared experience of human kindness. In the end, the journey of charity is one that we embark on together, enriching our lives and weaving a tapestry of compassion that spans the globe.

Chapter 4:
The Global View on Charity

In this interconnected world, charity isn't confined by geographic or cultural boundaries; it's a universal language that transcends all. Each corner of the globe has its unique traditions of giving, yet the core intention—to alleviate human suffering and improve the quality of life—remains a constant, echoing the same empathetic heartbeats from bustling cities to serene villages. Delving into the global view on charity, we uncover how diverse cultures contribute to a rich tapestry of philanthropy, guided by values that, despite their varied expressions, aim towards a shared goal of human betterment. Policies, too, play a significant role, shaping the landscape of giving through laws and incentives that encourage generosity. As we explore the varied ways societies support their members, we're reminded of the power of collective action. In doing so, we're not just observing the vast ecosystem of charity; we're invited to take our place within it, inspired to contribute our thread to the ever-expanding tapestry. This global perspective isn't just about understanding where and how charity happens—it's about recognizing our role within this global community, inspiring us to act with intention and heart, wherever we may be.

Different Cultures, Same Intentions

The notion that charity is a universal virtue, transcending boundaries, languages, and traditions, couldn't be clearer than in the diverse ways through which different cultures engage in acts of kindness and giving.

Across the globe, from the communal spirit of Ubuntu in Africa that emphasizes mutual support within the community, to the practice of Zakat in the Islamic faith, which mandates giving a portion of one's wealth to the needy, the core intent remains steadfastly the same: to uplift, to aid, and to connect on a profoundly human level. In the West, philanthropy often takes on a structured form with tax-deductible donations and charitable foundations, while in Eastern traditions, acts of charity are deeply interwoven with spiritual practices and the pursuit of karma. Despite these varied expressions, the drive to make a positive impact on another's life cuts across cultural divides, showcasing a remarkable global consensus on the value of compassion and generosity. This chapter delves into how cultures around the world embrace charity, not as a duty, but as a heartfelt commitment to bettering the human condition, reminding us that in the fabric of global society, our intentions to help one another are beautifully aligned.

The Influence of Policy on Charity In the pulsating heart of our global society, policies enacted by governments stand as critical waypoints that either bolster the charitable impulses of people or, unfortunately sometimes, divert these noble streams into stymied rivulets. To understand charity, to truly grasp its essence and the natural human inclination towards generosity, one must consider the compelling facets of policy and its undeniable impact on charitable actions.

Charity, in its most unadulterated form, transcends the mere act of giving. It's an expression of our collective humanity, a bridge that spans across the chasms created by inequality, hardship, and disaster. Yet, the path of this bridge is heavily guided by the policies and regulatory frameworks established by nations. These policies can either serve as strong support beams, encouraging the flow of aid and resources, or as barriers that restrict and confine that very flow.

Consider, for a moment, the impact of tax policies on charitable donations. Countries that offer tax incentives for donations to charitable organizations witness a significant increase in the volume and frequency of giving. These incentives not only encourage the act of giving but also bolster the financial health of charities, enabling them to expand their reach and enhance their impact. On the flip side, stringent tax regulations or lack of incentives can dampen the spirit of philanthropy, making it imperative for policymakers to craft laws that encourage and amplify charitable deeds.

Beyond tax policies, government grants and funding play a pivotal role in the ecosystem of charity. Strategic allocation of funds to non-profit organizations and charitable causes can catalyze efforts aimed at alleviating poverty, advancing education, and improving public health. Such support not only magnifies the impact of existing charities but also encourages the establishment of new organizations aimed at addressing niche problems within society.

However, the relationship between policy and charity is not solely one of financial transaction. Regulatory frameworks governing the operation of non-profit organizations significantly influence their efficiency, transparency, and accountability. Policies that demand rigorous auditing, transparent reporting, and ethical operations instill confidence in donors, ensuring that every penny donated is a penny toward making a tangible difference. Conversely, lenient regulations might pave the way for malpractice, diminishing public trust in charitable organizations and subsequently affecting the willingness to give.

International aid presents another dimension where policy critically impacts charity. The ease with which aid crosses borders can mean the difference between life and death in crisis situations. Policies favoring international cooperation and streamlined processes for the delivery of aid can significantly enhance the global response to natural disasters, epidemics, and famine. International partnerships, bolstered by supportive policies, enable a unified approach to global challenges, promoting the sharing of resources, knowledge, and expertise.

Moreover, policies aimed at protecting the rights and dignity of those in need — ensuring that aid is delivered in a manner that is respectful, efficient, and devoid of exploitation — are vital. These policies cement the ethical foundation upon which charity is built, affirming our collective responsibility towards our fellow beings.

The digital age has ushered in a new frontier of charitable giving. Policies that advocate for digital innovation within the charitable sector can lead to groundbreaking approaches to philanthropy. Blockchain technology, for instance, offers unparalleled transparency in transactions, enabling donors to track the journey of their contribution from wallet to cause. Policies that embrace these technologies and integrate them into the charitable landscape can redefine the efficacy and impact of charity.

However, the specter of overregulation looms large. Policies that are overly bureaucratic or restrictive can stifle the spirit of innovation within the charitable sector, binding it in red tape and slowing the pace at which aid reaches those in need. It's a delicate balance, where policies must provide a structured framework for operation without curbing the innate flexibility and responsiveness of charitable organizations.

Environmental policies also indirectly influence charity. As we face the escalating crisis of climate change, policies that encourage sustainable practices and support for environmental conservation can inspire charitable initiatives focused on protecting the planet. Charitable organizations that align with these goals receive a boost, both in terms of public support and policy backing, enabling them to contribute more effectively towards a sustainable future.

Education policy, too, plays a critical role. By ensuring that charitable efforts in education — from building schools to providing scholarships — are aligned with national education strategies, policies can amplify the impact of these initiatives. Such alignment ensures that charitable efforts are not just generous acts but strategic contributions to the nation's future.

At its core, the synergy between policy and charity reflects the broader societal acknowledgment of our interconnectedness and shared responsibility for each other's well-being. Policies that nurture charity echo a society's commitment to compassion, empathy, and action. As citizens and as human beings, understanding this relationship empowers us to advocate for policies that support charity, thereby amplifying our collective capacity to make a difference.

As we navigate the evolving landscape of modern society, it becomes increasingly clear that charity and policy must walk hand in hand. The challenges we face, both local and global, require not just the generous hearts of individuals but the deliberate, supportive framework of policies that encourage, protect, and multiply the impact of charitable endeavors.

Therefore, the journey towards a more charitable society is not just about encouraging individual philanthropy but also about advocating for policy changes that acknowledge and bolster the fundamental role of charity. It's about recognizing that in the grand narrative of human progress, the policies we enact are the soil in which the seeds of charity must flourish.

In conclusion, the influence of policy on charity is profound and multifaceted. As we strive to understand charity and the need to lend a helping hand, let us also advocate for policies that create a nurturing environment for charitable acts to thrive. Together, through thoughtful policy-making and heartfelt generosity, we can forge a future where charity in its truest, most impactful form becomes a defining feature of our society.

Chapter 5:
Charity Begins at Home: Fostering Generosity in the Family

As we navigate the complexities of instilling deep, meaningful values within the sanctuary of our homes, the concept of charity stands out not only as a moral compass but as a beacon of hope and understanding for the younger generation. It's within the family nucleus that the seeds of generosity are sown, watered by the acts and attitudes of those they look up to most. This crucial chapter delves into how families can be the foundational platform for fostering a spirit of giving that resonates far beyond the walls of the home. Through a blend of thoughtful actions, open discussions about the importance of helping others, and embedding these values into the everyday fabric of family life, we unveil the potential for creating a ripple effect of kindness. At its core, teaching children about charity equips them not only with the understanding that their actions can positively impact the world but also nurtures empathy, compassion, and a deep-rooted sense of responsibility towards others.

Yet, it's vital to recognize that the lessons of generosity and compassion start not with grand gestures, but with the simple, everyday moments that define our lives. A kind word here, a small act of helping there; it's these moments that accumulate, creating a powerful narrative for children to observe, learn, and eventually embody. As families embark on this journey together, the "echo" of their generosity reverberates, touching lives and making a tangible difference in the world. This is the essence of the notion that charity indeed begins at home, setting the stage for a lifelong pursuit of giving, understanding, and most importantly, love. With this foundation, we witness the transformation of individual acts of kindness into a collective movement of compassion and generosity that stands as a testament to the power and impact of nurturing these values within the family.

Teaching Children about Charity

Inculcating the spirit of giving in the hearts and minds of our young ones is perhaps the most profound legacy we can leave behind. Children are naturally inclined to be generous but guiding them to understand and practice charity can shape them into empathetic, understanding adults who recognize the importance of offering a hand when necessary. It starts with simple acts of sharing and caring within the family. Narrating stories of people in different circumstances helps them to view the world through a broader lens, nurturing a sense of global empathy. Encouraging small acts of kindness, like donating part of their allowance to a cause they care about or involving them in community service, sets a foundation for a lifelong commitment to helping others. It's about showing them that their actions, no matter how small, can make a significant difference in someone else's life. This chapter acknowledges that teaching charity isn't just about telling kids what to do; it's about leading by example and demonstrating that generosity isn't an obligation but a choice that enriches our lives, making the world a little brighter, one act of kindness at a time.

The Ripple Effect of Kindness

Within the confines of our homes, amidst the daily routines and the chaos of life, lies the potential for a profound impact that extends far beyond the walls that contain it. The act of instilling generosity within the family unit is not merely an exercise in morality; it becomes the epicenter of a ripple effect that can touch the lives of countless individuals. This section endeavors to explore the expansive reach of kindness that begins within the home, tracing its journey as it expands outward into the community and beyond.

It's integral to comprehend that every act of kindness, no matter its perceived size, holds within it an untapped potential to initiate change. Imagine a single act, as simple as teaching a child the value of sharing, then watching as this lesson is carried forward, adopted, and adapted by others. This is not merely hypothetical; it is the reality of kindness's ripple effect.

Kindness begets kindness; this is a truth universally acknowledged yet often overlooked in its simplicity and power. When family members observe acts of charity and generosity within their own homes, they are more likely to replicate these actions in their inter-actions outside the home. Thus, the home becomes not just a place of refuge, but a launching pad for benevolence that permeates societal boundaries.

In a world rife with examples of indifference and hostility, the power of a single generous act can be the beacon of hope that counters despair. It teaches resilience in the face of adversity and compassion in the place of apathy. The lessons of kindness learned at home serve as the foundation upon which individuals can build a more empathetic world.

Consider the achievements of local heroes and global icons alike, many of whom credit their family environments with instilling in them the values of charity and service. Their stories serve as testament to the idea that an early education in kindness can elevate an individual from being a passive observer of injustice to an active participant in its eradication.

However, fostering a culture of generosity within the family does not occur in a vacuum. It requires intentional actions, conversations, and, most importantly, examples set by caregivers. Children, with their innate capacity for empathy, absorb these lessons, often reflecting them in their future endeavors and interactions.

Moreover, the ripple of kindness is not confined to the immediate social circle of one's family and friends. As it travels, it inspires strangers, communities, and even institutions, demonstrating that the influence of a single act of kindness can indeed be boundless.

Yet, what stands as the cornerstone of this ripple effect is accessibility. Kindness does not demand grand gestures; rather, it thrives on the simple, everyday acts that showcase humanity's capacity for compassion. It's in the small favors, the words of encouragement, and the gestures of understanding that the essence of kindness is truly captured.

From a practical standpoint, encouraging acts of kindness within the family can manifest in various forms. It could be as simple as volunteering together at local community centers, participating in fundraising activities, or simply helping a neighbor in need. These activities not only solidify bonds among family members but also reinforce the importance of looking beyond one's needs and contributing to the greater good.

Education plays a pivotal role in this process as well. Through open discussions about global issues, families can cultivate a sense of responsibility and awareness in children, teaching them to be mindful of their actions and their potential impact on others. It is through this awareness that the seeds of empathy and charity are sown, eventually blossoming into actions that spearhead change.

Thus, the ripple effect of kindness, once set in motion, has the potential to transcend geographical, cultural, and social divides. It's a testament to the interconnectedness of humanity and the indelible impact of our collective actions. In understanding this, one realizes that the pursuit of kindness is not solely for the benefit of others but is intrinsically rewarding as well.

The narrative of kindness is one that is continuously written, with each chapter influenced by the preceding ones. Within this narrative, the family unit is the prologue, setting the tone for the stories of generosity and benevolence that follow. It is a reminder that in the grand tapestry of human existence, every thread of kindness is integral to the overall design.

In light of this, it becomes clear that the act of fostering a culture of kindness within the family is not just an act of charity; it is an investment in a future where empathy, compassion, and generosity are the defining traits of society. It underscores the belief that even the smallest act of kindness can spark a movement, transforming the world one ripple at a time.

As we navigate the complexities of life, let us remember the power that lies in kindness. Let it be the compass that guides our actions, the beacon that lights our path, and the legacy we choose to leave behind. For in the end, it is not through grand achievements that our lives are measured, but by the ripples of kindness we set in motion, whose waves touch the shores of countless hearts and souls.

Chapter 6:
The Faces of Charity

In this chapter, we dive into the heart of charity—its human aspect. Charity isn't merely an act; it's a symphony of stories, emotions, and transformations. It wears countless faces, from the humble volunteer at a local food bank to the philanthropic giants whose foundations span continents. Yet, the essence remains the same: a sincere attempt to make the world a better place. As we unravel personal tales of hope and help, we see how acts of kindness can ripple through communities, fostering a culture of generosity that transcends borders. From local heroes dedicating their lives to bettering their neighborhoods to global icons leveraging their influence for broad-scale change, each story adds a brushstroke to the larger picture of charity. These narratives are not just inspirational; they serve as a testament to the power of human compassion and the profound impact it can have. Understanding these faces of charity allows us to grasp the depth and breadth of generosity, motivating us to play our part in this vast network of care and support. As we explore these stories, it's clear that charity takes on many forms, but the outcome remains unwavering—a world where kindness is the foundational block of our society.

Personal Stories of Hope and Help

In the myriad landscape of human empathy and generosity, personal stories of hope and help stand as beacons of what we can achieve when we extend our hands towards those in need. Within these narratives, we find not just the beneficiaries of charity, but the remarkable transformation of the givers themselves. One might encounter the story of a single mother who, against all odds, found support from a stranger, turning her life around and setting a chain of goodwill in motion. Another tale may introduce a retiree who discovered purpose in tutoring underprivileged children, witnessing their lives unfurl towards brighter futures. These stories, rich with emotional depth and resonance, underscore a profound truth about giving: it is a two-way street that enriches the soul and weaves the fabric of our communities tighter. They remind us that behind every act of kindness, there's a face, a name, and a story, transforming abstract notions of charity into palpable human connections. So, as we delve into these personal stories, let's remember that each narrative not only showcases the resilience of the human spirit but also calls us to action, inviting us to become part of someone else's story of hope and help.

From Local Heroes to Global Icons Transitioning from being a locally known figure to a globally recognized icon in the sphere of charity is no small feat. It requires not just a deep commitment to a cause, but also the ability to inspire and mobilize across cultures and borders. The stories of those who have made this leap are not just tales of personal achievement but beacons of hope, illustrating the immense power of compassionate action to transcend geography and connect humanity.

The journey often begins in a moment of profound personal connection to an issue, a moment where a person sees a problem and decides that they cannot simply stand by. This decision, fueled by deep empathy and a sense of responsibility, sets them on a path that eventually impacts millions. Their initial steps, though small and local, are the start of a much larger journey.

Consider the example of individuals who start by addressing homelessness in their local community. They might begin by volunteering at a shelter, or by starting a small nonprofit to provide meals. These actions, though localized, are the seeds from which larger movements grow. As they share their stories and the narratives of those they help, they attract more support, enabling their efforts to expand.

The digital era has further democratized the process of becoming a global icon. Platforms such as social media, blogs, and crowdfunding have become invaluable tools for charity advocates. They allow local heroes to share their cause with a global audience, engaging directly with supporters around the world.

An essential ingredient in this transition is the story itself. Stories that resonate on a human level, that highlight shared values and common struggles, have the power to galvanize a global community. It's not just about raising funds, but about raising awareness and fostering a deep connection with the issue at hand.

As these local heroes gain traction on the global stage, their approach to charity begins to evolve. They become more strategic, leveraging their platform to not only draw attention to specific issues but to advocate for systemic changes. They collaborate with international organizations, governments, and businesses to address the root causes of the issues they're fighting against.

However, with increased visibility comes increased scrutiny. Global charity icons must navigate the complex and often politically charged landscape of international aid. They must be transparent about their methods, accountable for their actions, and genuinely committed to their cause.

This is where ethics play a critical role. Successful transitions from local hero to global icon are marked by an unwavering commitment to integrity. This means ensuring that actions align with the charity's mission, that funds are used effectively, and that the communities being helped are genuinely benefiting.

One of the most remarkable aspects of those who make this transition is their ability to maintain their grassroots ethos. Despite operating on a global stage, they remain deeply connected to the communities they serve. They listen to the needs of these communities and ensure they are not just providing aid but empowering individuals.

Education becomes a two-way street. While these icons educate the world about their cause, they also remain learners, constantly adapting to new information and changing situations. This humility and adaptability are key to their ongoing success.

The impact of transitioning from a local hero to a global icon in the world of charity extends beyond the immediate benefits to the causes they champion. They serve as proof that individual action can lead to global change. They inspire others to take up their own causes, showing that with passion and perseverance, it's possible to make a significant impact.

Moreover, these icons often pave the way for others. They prove that barriers such as location, background, or resources can be overcome. They show that change is possible when we're willing to take that first step, however small it may seem at the time.

Technology continues to play a pivotal role in this transition. Innovations in communication, fundraising, and project management have made it easier than ever for local heroes to project their message on a global stage. As technology evolves, so too will the ways in which these icons can connect with and inspire the world.

It's important to note, however, that the journey from a local advocate to a global icon in charity is not a solo endeavor. It requires the support of a community - both the local community that first inspires action and the global community that rallies around the cause. This support network is crucial, providing not just the funds, but the moral and logistical support needed to navigate the complexities of global charity work.

In conclusion, the transformation from local heroes to global icons in the charity space is a multifaceted journey, marked by humility, resilience, and a deep commitment to making a difference. These individuals remind us that with passion and perseverance, we can indeed change the world. They stand as testaments to the power of charity, inspiring each of us to consider how we might contribute, in our way, to the global tapestry of kindness and support.

Chapter 7:
Navigating the Challenges of Charity

Embarking on charitable efforts comes with its own set of hurdles, presenting a tapestry of complexities that require both heart and strategy to navigate successfully. While the instinct to help is a noble one, it's crucial to approach charity with a mindful awareness of the potential pitfalls. A critical element is resisting the 'saviour complex,' a well-intentioned but often counterproductive mindset that overlooks the importance of empowering those in need to help themselves. This chapter delves into strategies for avoiding such pitfalls, emphasizing the need for sustainable assistance that respects the agency and dignity of beneficiaries. It's about striking a delicate balance, ensuring that the help offered today doesn't inadvertently undermine the recipient's autonomy tomorrow. Through the careful consideration of these challenges, we unlock the full potential of charitable actions not just to provide immediate relief, but to foster a framework of support that encourages long-term self-sufficiency and resilience. The journey of charity, fraught with obstacles though it may be, is also ripe with opportunities for learning, growth, and the deepening of our collective humanity.

Avoiding the Saviour Complex

In the intricate dance of giving and receiving, it's crucial to tread carefully to avoid the pitfall of the saviour complex—a mindset where the giver views themselves as the sole rescuer of those in need. This complex, while rooted in the desire to help, often oversimplifies the complexities of poverty, need, and helplessness, inadvertently undermining the dignity and agency of those being helped. Instead of positioning ourselves as the heroes in someone else's story, it's more productive and respectful to see aid as a partnership. True change occurs when help is delivered not from a pedestal but from a place of humility and solidarity. We must embrace the notion that those we aim to assist have strengths, capabilities, and insights invaluable to their own empowerment process. By fostering a reciprocal relationship based on mutual respect, we not only amplify the impact of our charitable endeavors but also enrich our own lives with deeper understanding and genuine connection.

Ensuring Sustainable Help In the realm of charity, the bridge between intent and impact is built on the foundation of sustainability. Providing aid that endures long after the initial intervention is crucial, particularly in a world where temporary solutions often create deeper dependencies rather than genuine empowerment. It's not just about offering a hand but ensuring that the hand can eventually support itself.

Looking through the prism of history, we've seen the ramifications of well-meant aid that fails to consider the future. Communities become reliant on external support, creating cycles that are hard to break. The task at hand, then, is to foster environments where individuals and communities can flourish independently. This means investing in education, local economies, and infrastructure in ways that are mindful of cultural identities and environmental sustainability.

One of the key strategies for ensuring sustainable help is to listen. It seems simple, but the act of listening—to the needs, desires, and ideas of those we aim to help—is often overlooked. Real sustainability comes from solutions that are designed with, and not just for, the beneficiary communities. This participatory approach empowers individuals, giving them a stake in their own development journey.

An investment in local leadership is another cornerstone of sustainable help. By nurturing local talent and leadership, charitable endeavors can create a legacy of empowerment that lasts well beyond their direct involvement. It's about passing the baton in a race towards self-sufficiency, enabling communities to address their own needs and challenges in the long run.

Furthermore, the intersection of technology and charity offers unprecedented opportunities for sustainable help. Digital platforms can provide access to education and resources that were previously out of reach. By leveraging technology, charities can not only broaden their impact but also create systems that communities can independently manage and evolve.

Monitoring and evaluation are also pivotal in the realm of sustainable charity. These processes allow us to see what works and, just as importantly, what doesn't. By learning from each endeavor, charities can refine their approaches, ensuring that their help is not just effective in the moment but also sustainable over time.

To truly ensure sustainability, we must also consider the environmental impact of charitable activities. Projects that support renewable energy, water conservation, and sustainable agriculture can provide communities with the tools they need for long-term resilience in the face of climate change and resource scarcity.

Economic sustainability is another piece of the puzzle. Initiatives that promote entrepreneurship, financial literacy, and access to markets can transform communities from aid recipients to economic contributors. These kinds of programs not only foster independence but also contribute to global economic diversity and strength.

Partnerships are invaluable in the pursuit of sustainable help. Collaborations between charities, governments, businesses, and local communities can pool resources and knowledge, making way for more robust, lasting solutions. These alliances can amplify impact, making the seemingly insurmountable, surmountable.

On a larger scale, policy advocacy is integral to sustainability. By influencing policies that affect aid, charity, and development, organizations can help dismantle systemic barriers to self-reliance. This means not just giving a fish or teaching how to fish but also ensuring that the pond is well-stocked and accessible to all.

At the heart of ensuring sustainable help is the understanding that charity is not just a response to immediate needs but also a long-term commitment to building a better world. It's about planting seeds that will grow into forests, providing shade and sustenance for generations to come.

Tackling the complex issues that prevent sustainable help requires innovation, persistence, and a willingness to learn and adapt. There's no one-size-fits-all solution, but with targeted efforts and a holistic approach, significant progress can be made.

It's essential to recognize that the journey towards sustainable help is a shared one. Each of us has a role to play, whether as donors, volunteers, activists, or policymakers. By coming together with a common purpose, we can create waves of change that extend far beyond our individual actions.

Finally, it's worth noting that ensuring sustainable help is an ongoing process. The world is constantly changing, bringing new challenges and opportunities. Staying committed to the principles of sustainability, learning from our experiences, and being willing to adapt our strategies are crucial for continued success.

As we forge ahead, let us remember that the true measure of our efforts lies not just in the help we provide today but in the lasting impact we create for tomorrow. Sustainable help is more than a goal—it's a promise, a commitment to a future where everyone has the opportunity to thrive.

Chapter 8:
Technology and Charity: The New Frontier

As we navigate through the digital era, the landscape of charitable giving and engagement is undergoing a monumental transformation. The burgeoning synergy between technology and charity is not just reshaping how we give, but also expanding the reach and impact of philanthropic efforts. We've moved beyond the traditional methods of fundraising and awareness campaigns into a realm where a single tweet, share, or like can mobilize thousands, if not millions, to rally for a cause. This new frontier is characterized by its immediacy, inclusivity, and innovation. Crowdfunding platforms are empowering individuals from all walks of life to initiate and contribute to causes close to their hearts, effectively democratizing the process of philanthropy. The digital age is dismantling barriers, making it easier for anyone with an internet connection to not only learn about the struggles of distant communities but to also contribute in meaningful ways. However, this shift isn't without its challenges; as we embrace this new paradigm, it's essential to navigate it thoughtfully, ensuring that technology amplifies the essence of charity—compassion, empathy, and the desire to make a difference. By leveraging technology wisely, we can open doors to unprecedented opportunities for charitable endeavors, ultimately fostering a more connected and empathetic world.

How the Internet is Changing the Way We Give

In an age where the digital world has become an extension of our physical one, the internet is revolutionizing the landscape of charity, reshaping how we connect, empathize, and ultimately, give back. Gone are the days when giving was confined to the wealthy, the churches, or the philanthropic elite. Today, the power of a simple click brings together a global community of givers, eager to support causes dear to their hearts from thousands of miles away. The advent of online donations, social media campaigns, and crowdfunding platforms means that anyone with internet access can contribute to making a tangible difference, be it by donating, sharing information, or rallying support for those in need. This shift not only democratizes the act of giving but also amplifies the impact we can have as a collective force. It encourages a culture of openness and transparency, where the stories of those we help are shared, creating a cycle of generosity fueled by the visible outcomes of our contributions. As we navigate this new frontier, it's essential to embrace these changes with a spirit of innovation and compassion, heralding a future where giving is not just an act of charity, but a fundamental part of our digital identity.

The Rise of Crowdfunding As we navigate through the digital age, the landscape of charity and giving is being remarkably transformed by the surge of crowdfunding. This innovative approach has democratised philanthropy, breaking down traditional barriers and creating a direct line between those in need and those willing to help. Crowdfunding has leveraged the power of the internet to rally support for causes, both big and small, pulling together resources from a global pool of donors.

At its core, crowdfunding represents a shift in how we conceptualize aid and support. It transcends geographical limitations, allowing individuals from any corner of the world to contribute to a cause that resonates with them. This evolution in giving reflects the broader changes in our society, where connectivity and immediacy are valued.

The beauty of crowdfunding lies in its simplicity and accessibility. Anyone with a compelling story and a need can launch a campaign, relying on the strength of their narrative to gather support. This has opened up new avenues for individuals and small groups who previously had no platform to share their stories or seek aid. It's a testament to the power of collective small acts of kindness leading to monumental impacts.

Moreover, the transparency and accountability offered by most crowdfunding platforms provide reassurance to donors. They can often see exactly where their money is going and, in many cases, receive updates on the progress of the cause they've supported. This fosters a sense of connection and personal investment in the success of the project or relief effort, forging a more intimate link between donors and beneficiaries.

However, the rise of crowdfunding also reflects deeper societal shifts. As trust in traditional institutions wanes, people are turning more towards grassroots movements and direct action. Crowdfunding embodies this transition, empowering ordinary people to drive change and offer support without the intermediation of large organizations.

Yet, the popularity of crowdfunding also poses challenges. With so many campaigns vying for attention, it can be difficult for worthy causes to stand out. This has led to an increase in the professionalization of campaign strategies, with a focus on storytelling, social media engagement, and marketing techniques to capture public interest.

Despite these obstacles, the potential of crowdfunding as a force for good is undeniable. It has enabled remarkable stories of humanity and generosity to emerge, from funding life-saving medical treatments to supporting small businesses in crisis. These stories not only raise funds but also awareness, inspiring others to take action and contribute to the cycle of kindness.

The critical role of social media in the proliferation of crowdfunding cannot be overstated. Platforms such as Facebook, Twitter, and Instagram serve as vital conduits for sharing and discovering campaigns. The viral potential of these platforms means that a campaign can quickly garner widespread support, illustrating the strength of community and shared human values.

Furthermore, crowdfunding challenges the traditional power dynamics of charity. It places agency in the hands of those in need, allowing them to define their narratives and solutions. This empowerment aspect is a significant departure from the top-down approaches that have historically dominated the charity sector.

As crowdfunding continues to grow, it also evolves. We're seeing innovations that blend crowdfunding with other forms of financing, such as microloans and peer-to-peer lending, expanding the possibilities for support and development projects worldwide.

It's also leading to a deeper understanding and empathy towards global challenges. By presenting stories and causes from various cultures and communities, crowdfunding educates and informs, making distant issues feel close and relatable. This fosters a global mindset towards charity, breaking down parochial perspectives.

The future of crowdfunding in charity looks bright, with new technologies such as blockchain offering possibilities for even greater transparency and efficiency. As platforms continue to refine their processes and safeguards, the potential for fraud and misuse diminishes, making crowdfunding a more reliable and trustworthy avenue for philanthropy.

Yet, for all its benefits, the essence of crowdfunding remains rooted in the timeless human values of empathy, generosity, and solidarity. It's a reminder that in a world often marked by division, there exists a common desire to support one another, to lift each other up during times of need, and to collectively aspire for a better world.

In conclusion, the rise of crowdfunding in the realm of charity encapsulates a profound shift towards a more connected, immediate, and personal form of philanthropy. Its continued growth and evolution promise to reshape not just how we give, but how we think about the act of giving itself. As we look to the future, the principles and potential of crowdfunding hold the promise of fostering a more engaged, empathetic, and empowered world.

In embracing this shift, we're not just witnessing a change in the mechanics of charity; we're participating in a broader cultural movement that redefines the very essence of help and hope. It prompts us to reflect on the impact of our contributions, no matter how small, and challenges us to be proactive agents of change. This is the power and promise of crowdfunding—a testament to the unmistakable strength found in unity and shared purpose.

Chapter 9:
Corporate Social Responsibility:
When Business Gives Back

In an era when the spotlight on corporate behavior has intensified, companies around the globe are recognizing the indispensable role they play in the broader social fabric. Corporate Social Responsibility (CSR) is no longer a buzzword but a business imperative, ethically binding organizations to contribute positively to society. This chapter delves into how CSR transcends traditional corporate philanthropy, embedding social and environmental concerns in business operations and interactions with stakeholders. With a keen focus on the transformative power of ethical business practices, we explore concrete examples of effective CSR that not only bolster the company's image but also contribute substantially to societal welfare. By intertwining profit with purpose, forward-thinking companies are setting a benchmark for success that measures beyond financial gains, encompassing social, environmental, and economic impacts. The journey through this chapter aims to ignite a conviction that when businesses give back, they pave the way for a sustainable future where everyone thrives. It's a clarion call for organizations worldwide to harness their resources, innovation, and influence to make a profound difference in the world, challenging the status quo and reshaping the narrative around corporate responsibility. Through compelling narratives and demonstrative cases, we transcend the traditional view of charity, advocating for a model where businesses and communities grow hand in hand, fostering a world where generosity and compassion are not only expected but embodied in the very essence of business operations.

The Impact of Ethical Business Practices

In the heart of corporate social responsibility lies a compelling narrative about ethical business practices and their profound influence on communities and the broader society. Within these frameworks, companies not only pledge allegiance to profit but also to the principles of integrity, philanthropy, and sustainability, paving the way for a more empathetic world. It's a journey where every decision, no matter how minute, becomes a testament to the values a company holds dear, serving as a beacon of hope and a source of inspiration for others to follow. This path, fueled by the genuine desire to make a difference, demonstrates that businesses can and should be a force for good. By embedding ethical considerations into their operations, companies become key players in addressing societal challenges, promoting social justice, and inspiring a wave of change that reaches far beyond their immediate stakeholders. It's a powerful reminder that in the grand tapestry of life, every stitch counts, encouraging us to envision a world where business success and social welfare are not just parallel goals but are deeply interwoven into the fabric of our collective future.

Examples of Effective CSR

Corporate Social Responsibility (CSR) is more than just a company donating a sum of their profits at the end of the fiscal year. It's a testament to how businesses can thread compassion into the fabric of their operations, weaving positive impacts into the communities they serve. The heart of CSR lies in understanding that giving back is not just an act of charity—it's a means of driving meaningful change. Let's dive into examples that not only demonstrate the power of effective

CSR but also might inspire businesses to consider how they too can contribute to the greater good.

One of the standout examples is the global technology company that embarked on a mission to bring educational resources to underprivileged communities. The initiative wasn't just about donating gadgets and internet access; it was about creating sustainable methods for education, enabling teachers with the right tools, and providing students with a world of information. The company's commitment went beyond a one-time donation, focusing on long-term skill development that could uplift entire communities.

Another shining example is a multinational retail corporation that made it their mission to source products sustainarily. This wasn't merely an environmental stance. It impacted the very lives of the farmers and producers in developing countries, ensuring they were paid fair wages and worked in safe conditions. This approach proved that ethical business practices could create a ripple effect, benefiting ecosystems, economies, and individuals.

The success of a famous coffee chain in contributing to global water conservation efforts is something to behold. Recognizing the immense water usage in coffee production, the company invested in technology and farming practices designed to reduce water consumption. Through community partnerships and innovative technologies, they were able to save billions of gallons of water, showing that environmental responsibility and business can, indeed, go hand in hand.

In the realm of health care, a pharmaceutical giant took CSR to heart by providing affordable medicines to developing countries. Understanding that access to healthcare is a global issue, they devised programs to lower costs for critical medications in impoverished regions. Their efforts showcased how companies could play a crucial role in solving global health challenges.

The contributions of a renowned automotive company to foster innovation in clean energy are noteworthy. By openly sharing their electric vehicle patents, they encouraged other manufacturers to accelerate the development of sustainable transportation solutions. This bold move underscored the belief that competition should take a backseat when it comes to addressing climate change.

A consumer electronics leader's initiative to recycle and refurbish used gadgets has set a new standard for the industry. Not only does this program reduce electronic waste, but it also ensures that technology is accessible to those who might not afford brand-new products. This effort shows how CSR initiatives can be designed to address both environmental and social needs.

Then there's the story of a food and beverage conglomerate that focuses on empowering farmers by investing in agricultural education. By providing resources and knowledge on sustainable farming practices, they ensure long-term viability of farming communities and secure their own supply chain, perfectly illustrating how business interests and social responsibility can align.

The initiative of a global sports brand to improve factory conditions and ensure fair labor practices across its supply chain has not gone unnoticed. Transparency reports and CSR campaigns highlight the company's commitment to human rights and workplace safety, showcasing how brands can lead by example in ethical manufacturing.

An oil and gas corporation might not be the first entity you think of when considering CSR, but one in particular has made vast strides in renewable energy investments. Recognizing the need for a transition to more sustainable energy sources, they've committed billions towards the development of wind, solar, and biofuel technologies, proving that even the most traditional industries can pivot towards a more sustainable future.

Last but not least, a transportation network company's initiative to offer free or discounted rides to healthcare appointments for low-income individuals highlights the potential of CSR to directly impact people's lives. By leveraging their core services for social good, they provide a critical resource for those in need, demonstrating that CSR can be effectively integrated into the very business model of a company.

These examples serve not just as a beacon of hope but as a call to action for businesses worldwide. Effective CSR goes beyond charity; it's about embedding a sense of responsibility in every aspect of a business's operations. As consumers become more conscious of the social and environmental footprints of the companies they support, CSR is no longer optional—it's essential.

Through innovative thinking and a commitment to ethical practices, businesses can contribute to solving some of the world's most pressing issues. The examples mentioned are a testament to the power of corporate social responsibility. They underscore the fact that when companies align their resources and expertise with a cause, the impact can be monumental.

The journey of integrating CSR into the core of business operations is an ongoing process. It requires vision, leadership, and most importantly, a genuine desire to make a difference. Let these examples inspire and motivate companies to take up the mantle of responsibility, not just for the betterment of their brand but for the betterment of society as a whole.

In essence, CSR exemplifies how businesses can extend a helping hand, demonstrating that when corporations commit to doing good, the world takes notice. And in doing so, they not only enrich communities and protect the environment but they also pave the way for a new era of ethical business practices. It's a win-win for businesses, society, and the planet.

Chapter 10:
The Dark Side of Charity

In our journey through the essence and impact of charity, we've celebrated its virtues and acknowledged its power to transform lives. Yet, it's critical that we also confront the unsettling truths lurking in its shadows. The dark side of charity, though uncomfortable to face, is an essential chapter in understanding the complete narrative of giving. Misuse of funds and resources acts as a stark reminder that good intentions aren't always enough. Stories of well-meant donations misallocated or squandered can dishearten the most fervent philanthropists. However, this chapter isn't just a cautionary tale; it's a call to action. It's a prompt to dig deeper, to ask the hard questions, and to demand transparency from those who steward our contributions. Ensuring that your contribution counts isn't just a matter of due diligence; it's a testament to the respect we owe to the beneficiaries of our generosity. By embodying a more discerning and informed approach to charity, we not only safeguard our own intentions but also honor the trust placed in us by those we aim to help. Let this awareness not dishearten but empower us, for in understanding the pitfalls, we're better equipped to make a tangible, positive impact.

The Misuse of Funds and Resources

While the world of charity blooms with stories of hope and warmth, casting a shadow over its noble intentions is the problematic aspect of misuse. It's a bitter truth to swallow that not all funds and resources dedicated to charitable causes reach their intended destinations.

Mismanagement, sometimes cloaked in good intentions, other times in greed, diverts resources that could potentially change lives, solve community issues, or provide disaster relief. This deviation not only dampens the spirit of generosity among the populace but also erodes trust, making it crucial for every potential donor to wear a lens of scrutiny. It's vital to remember, however, that the actions of a few should not deter the collective momentum towards making a difference. The misallocation of funds and misutilization of resources serve as a call to action for more transparent, accountable, and ethical charity practices. As much as we are moved to give, we must also move with caution and wisdom, ensuring our contributions indeed light up the darkest corners of human need.

How to Ensure Your Contribution Counts In the dynamic and ever-expanding landscape of charitable endeavors, the importance of making sure that your contributions genuinely make an impact cannot be overstated. The landscape is filled with stories, both heartwarming tales of generosity reborn and cautionary tales of good intentions leading nowhere. As someone eager to make a difference, understanding how to navigate this space with wisdom and effecttiveness is pivotal.

At the heart of every impactful contribution is the principle of informed giving. In a world where information is at our fingertips, taking the time to research and understand the organizations or causes you are interested in supporting is crucial. This doesn't just include glancing at their website but digging deeper into their mission, projects, financials, and the population they serve. This due diligence ensures that your contribution, whether it's your time, money, or resources, ends up where it's most needed and can do the most good.

Another critical aspect is aligning your contributions with your values and passions. Philanthropy is most meaningful and sustainable when it resonates with your personal beliefs and areas of interest. This alignment not only amplifies the impact of your contribution but also enhances your personal satisfaction and commitment. Whether it's supporting education, alleviating poverty, or contributing to disaster relief, making sure your efforts align with your core values is key to a meaningful contribution.

Understanding the difference between immediate relief and long-term solutions is also important. Immediate relief provides necessary help in the wake of crises, but long-term solutions aim to address the root causes of issues. Striking a balance between supporting immediate needs and investing in sustainable solutions can maximize the impact of your contributions. Sometimes, this means supporting initiatives that build communities, foster independence, and create sustainable change.

Engagement beyond the checkbook counts significantly. In today's digital age, raising awareness, advocating for causes, and leveraging your network for support can amplify the impact of your contributions. It's about being an active participant in the cause you support, rather than a passive donor. This engagement can empower communities, inspire others to contribute, and create a ripple effect that extends far beyond your initial contribution.

Aligning with organizations that possess strong local connections and understanding is paramount. These organizations have the insight and relationships necessary to navigate complex cultural, political, and social landscapes. They know where help is most needed and how to deliver it in a way that is respectful, appropriate, and sustainable. Their local expertise ensures that contributions are not just well-intentioned but are also effective and welcomed by the communities they aim to serve.

Maintaining transparency and accountability in your contributions is non-negotiable. This means supporting organizations that are clear about their goals, strategies, expenditures, and achievements. They should have mechanisms in place for reporting their progress and be open to scrutiny. This transparency builds trust and reassures donors that their contributions are being used effectively to make a tangible impact.

The power of collective action cannot be ignored. Often, contributions can have a more significant impact when combined with the efforts of others. This can take the form of matching grant initiatives, collective fund drives, or community-based projects. Collaborating with others amplifies the reach and effectiveness of your contribution, making it part of a larger force for good.

Another often overlooked aspect is the importance of following up on your contributions. Staying informed about the progress and impact of your donations or volunteer work can provide valuable insights into the effectiveness of the support and help guide future contributions. This follow-up reinforces the connection between donor and cause, fostering a deeper understanding and commitment to the work being done.

Embracing flexibility and adaptability in your philanthropic endeavors is also crucial. The needs of communities and the challenges they face can change rapidly. Being open to adjusting your support to match shifting priorities ensures that your contributions remain relevant and impactful. It's about being responsive to the needs as they evolve, ensuring that your support continues to make a meaningful difference.

Remember, meaningful contributions often require patience and commitment. The most impactful changes rarely happen overnight but are the result of sustained effort and dedication. Embracing a long-term view of your philanthropic journey allows for deeper engagement with the causes you care about and fosters lasting change that can transform lives and communities.

Lastly, personal involvement and volunteering offer an unparalleled depth of understanding and connection to the causes you support. They provide a tangible sense of the challenges faced by those you're helping and offer personal growth opportunities. Through direct involvement, you can witness the direct impact of your contributions, adding a deeply human dimension to the notion of charity.

By integrating these principles into your philanthropic efforts, you ensure that your contributions make a significant and lasting impact. The journey of charity is one of continual learning, engagement, and commitment. It's not just about offering a helping hand but about making a real difference in the world. Your contributions, guided by knowledge, aligned with passion, and executed with precision, can indeed count in ways you never imagined possible.

As we move towards a more interconnected and compassionate world, the act of giving transforms into an even more powerful force. One that not just alleviates immediate needs but fosters a culture of kindness, empathy, and shared humanity. Let your contributions be a testament to the belief that every act of generosity, no matter its size, shapes a better world for us all.

In summary, ensuring your contribution counts is an active, ongoing process that demands thoughtfulness, engagement, and commitment. It's about being informed, aligned with your values, and active in your approach. It's a process of continuous learning and adaptation, but most importantly, it's about making a meaningful difference. Through thoughtful, informed, and engaged philanthropy, you can ensure that your contributions not only count but change lives.

Chapter 11:
Volunteerism: The Backbone of Charitable Endeavors

At its core, volunteerism embodies the spirit of selflessness, standing tall as the pillar supporting the vast edifice of charity. In this era where individual actions can ripple across communities and even borders, volunteering has never been more crucial. It's not merely about lending a hand; it's about weaving a tapestry of hope, one thread at a time. The ethos of giving one's time, skills, and energy without expecting anything in return strengthens the foundation of charitable endeavors, transforming the act of giving into a powerful catalyst for change. What makes volunteerism so remarkable is its capacity to unite people from diverse backgrounds towards a common goal of alleviating suffering, addressing societal issues, and building resilient communities. This nurturing of empathy and mutual respect is what bridges the gap between mere existence and meaningful life. As we navigate the intricate landscape of charity, it becomes evident that without the volunteers' unwavering commitment and infectious enthusiasm, many success stories would remain untold. Thus, in shedding light on the exceptional role of volunteerism, we're not only acknowledging its value but are also called to action. The journey of a thousand miles begins with a single step, and that step is yours to take. By finding the right opportunity and understanding the manifold benefits of volunteering, we each have the power to contribute to a legacy of kindness, one that will echo through the ages.

Finding the Right Opportunity

Finding the right volunteering opportunity is akin to discovering a hidden gem that aligns perfectly with your skills and passion. It's about connecting your desire to help with actions that make a tangible difference. Imagine a world where everyone's efforts slot in seamlessly with the needs of those around them, creating a tapestry of change and hope. It starts with self-reflection; understanding what excites you, what causes tug at your heartstrings, and how much time you can dedicate. Then, it's research time, exploring the vast landscape of charitable organizations to find one whose mission resonates with your core values. Don't hesitate to reach out, ask questions, and even participate in events or short-term projects to get a feel for the organization's impact. Remember, the perfect volunteering opportunity not only benefits those you aim to help but enriches your life, broadening your understanding of the world, and knitting you closer to the global community. This journey towards finding where you belong in the realm of volunteerism is not just fulfilling; it's transformative, paving the way for a legacy of generosity etched in the lives of those you touch.

The Benefits of Volunteering As our journey through the realms of charity continues, we arrive at a crucial juncture that bridges personal initiative with communal impact: volunteering. This act, seemingly simple, embodies a profound generosity of spirit that echoes through the lives of countless individuals and communities. Let's delve into the manifold benefits of volunteering, not only to those we help but also to ourselves.

At its core, volunteering fosters a deep sense of connection. In an era where digital screens often mediate relationships, the direct, human-to-human interactions facilitated by volunteer work stand out as bastions of genuine connection. This form of engagement brings people together, uniting them under a common cause and diminishing the barriers that societal constructs often erect.

Moreover, volunteering serves as a powerful antidote to the feelings of isolation and loneliness that pervade modern society. By stepping out and offering a hand, volunteers inevitably find themselves part of a community. This community, bound by the drive to make a difference, provides a sense of belonging and purpose that many seek.

On a psychological level, the act of giving back through volunteering can significantly boost mental health. Engaging in charitable activities has been linked to reduced levels of stress and depression, as well as an increase in self-esteem. The act of helping others triggers the release of serotonin, a neurotransmitter responsible for feelings of happiness and well-being.

Volunteering also presents an invaluable opportunity for skill development. Whether organizing events, managing projects, or providing direct aid, volunteers often find themselves navigating challenges that foster growth. These experiences not only enhance personal and professional skills but also enrich one's resume, showcasing a commitment to community and personal initiative.

The educational benefits of volunteering cannot be overstated. It offers a hands-on learning experience that textbooks and lectures struggle to replicate. Volunteers gain insights into societal issues, understanding not just the challenges but also the potential solutions that can make a tangible difference.

Another aspect worth highlighting is the potential for career exploration. Volunteering allows individuals to sample various fields without the commitment required by formal employment. This can be particularly enlightening for students and those considering career changes, providing a glimpse into possible futures.

From a health perspective, volunteering has been associated with physical benefits as well. Studies suggest that those who volunteer regularly may enjoy longer lifespans, improved heart health, and decreased risk of chronic diseases. It seems that the act of giving back is not just good for the soul but also for the body.

At an individual level, volunteering cultivates empathy and compassion. By witnessing the struggles and resilience of others, volunteers develop a deeper understanding of the human condition. This heightened awareness fosters a more empathetic and inclusive worldview, impacting not just how individuals act but how they encourage others to act as well.

Volunteering also plays a key role in strengthening communities. Volunteers often act as the glue that holds communities together, responding to needs swiftly and effectively. Through their efforts, they can transform neighborhoods, making them safer, healthier, and more vibrant places to live.

For young people, volunteering offers a constructive way to navigate their own identities and values. It provides a platform for activism and advocacy, empowering them to effect change on issues they're passionate about. In doing this, it fosters a sense of agency and responsibility towards shaping a better world.

On a larger scale, volunteering is an engine for social change. It mobilizes resources and human capital towards addressing societal challenges, often filling gaps that governmental and private sectors cannot. Through collective action, volunteers have the power to enact systemic changes, challenging the status quo and inspiring hope.

Furthermore, volunteering promotes cultural exchange and understanding. In a world that's increasingly globalized yet divided, volunteer initiatives that cross borders foster a sense of global citizenship. Participants learn about different cultures, languages, and ways of life, widening their perspectives and challenging their preconceptions.

Lastly, the transformative power of volunteering extends to those who are on the receiving end of charitable efforts. Beyond the immediate relief or support provided, these acts of kindness inspire a cycle of giving. Beneficiaries are often motivated to pay it forward, perpetuating a ripple effect of generosity that transcends time and space.

As we reflect on the numerous benefits of volunteering, it becomes clear that this act of service is far more than a one-way street. It is a dynamic exchange—a gift that enriches both giver and receiver, weaving together the fabric of society with threads of compassion and resilience. In embracing the spirit of volunteerism, we step into a world where every individual has the power to make a difference. Let this knowledge empower us to take action, to reach out, and to contribute to the tapestry of human kindness that connects us all.

Chapter 12:
The Future of Charity

In the evolving landscape of benevolence, the future of charity holds an exhilarating promise. As we navigate past the challenges and triumphs detailed in previous chapters, we can't help but look forward with optimism to the innovations and cultural shifts lying on the horizon. The coming years will likely witness an unprecedented fusion of technology and human compassion, bringing to life novel ways of giving that we could barely imagine a decade ago. We're not just talking about digital wallets and crowdfunding platforms, but a deeper, more ingrained culture of kindness that transcends geographical and societal barriers. Imagine a world where giving is seamlessly integrated into our daily lives, where the act of charity is not a separate endeavor but a continuous, fluid part of our existence. This future is not only attainable but necessary. As we strive towards building this new culture, it becomes increasingly clear that the essence of charity—our shared humanity—is what truly binds us. The path ahead is ripe with potential to redefine not just how we give, but why we give, fostering a global community that prioritizes compassion and understanding above all else. The journey towards this future starts with each one of us today, committing to small acts of kindness that, collectively, can transform the world.

Innovations in Giving

As we delve into the ever-evolving landscape of charity, it's clear that the spirit of giving is undergoing a transformative shift, spurred by the latest technological advancements. For centuries, the act of giving was a straightforward transaction, often limited by geographical boundaries and the lack of immediate communication. Fast forward to today, and we find ourselves in an era where philanthropy is no longer just about writing checks or donating physical items. The digital realm has ushered in an age of *innovations in giving*, making it possible for anyone with internet access to contribute to causes they're passionate about, regardless of their location. From blockchain technology ensuring transparency in transactions to social media platforms amplifying the reach of charitable campaigns, these advancements are reshaping our approach to helping others. Moreover, the rise of virtual volunteering opportunities allows individuals to offer their skills and time without the need for physical presence, breaking down the barriers that once hindered widespread participation. As we embrace these changes, it's essential to remember that at the heart of innovation lies the age-old desire to make a difference in the lives of others. By leveraging the tools and platforms at our disposal, we're not only expanding the scope of who can give but also how we can give, fostering a more inclusive and interconnected world of philanthropy.

Building a Culture of Kindness As we journey further into the complexities and sheer scope of what charity entails, we find ourselves standing on the cusp of a transformative idea. It's not merely about the acts of giving or the occasional gesture of help. It's about instilling a pervasive, lasting ethos of kindness within our societies. Picture a world where the default reaction to seeing someone in need is to help; where corporations not only aim for profit but for positive impact; where the next generation grows up understanding the intrinsic value of giving. This is the essence of building a culture of kindness.

Firstly, it's essential to acknowledge that kindness is a choice, an intentional act that stems from the belief in the value of other people's well-being. It begins with individuals and their daily interactions.

Imagine if each person decided to perform just one act of kindness each day. The cumulative effect of these acts could be revolutionary, transforming our interactions and, eventually, our communities.

Creating such a culture requires awareness and education. Schools play a pivotal role in this regard. Integrating lessons on empathy, charity, and the broader social impacts of kindness into the curriculum can mold young minds to naturally incline towards helping others. Education, however, should not stop at school. Lifelong learning about the virtues of kindness and charity, coupled with the understanding of their profound impact, can keep the culture thriving across all ages.

In addition to education, the power of storytelling cannot be underestimated in building a culture of kindness. Personal stories of hope, resilience, and the positive outcomes of charitable acts have a unique ability to inspire and motivate. They remind us that our actions, no matter how small, can make a significant difference in someone else's life.

Moreover, technology and social media play a critical role in today's society. They have the power to amplify acts of kindness, spreading positive stories and making it easier for people to find ways to help. Platforms that connect volunteers with opportunities or facilitate crowdfunding for those in need can turn the desire to help into concrete action.

Corporations and businesses also hold a key to nurturing a culture of kindness. Corporate social responsibility (CSR) is not just a buzzword but a practice that can lead to substantial societal benefits. When businesses commit to ethical practices, give back to their communities, and place people over profit, they set a powerful example for others to follow.

At the community level, developing a culture of kindness means being proactive in recognizing and addressing the needs around us. Community centers, religious organizations, and local nonprofits can serve as hubs of kindness, enabling people to contribute their time, resources, and skills to help others. These institutions can organize regular community service days, kindness challenges, and charity drives, making it easier for everyone to participate in fostering a culture of kindness.

However, building such a culture isn't without its challenges. The key to overcoming these obstacles lies in perseverance and the belief in the cascading effect of kindness. Challenges such as apathy, skepticism, and the misconception that one person's effort can't make a difference can be mitigated by continuously highlighting and celebrating acts of kindness, no matter how small.

Similarly, avoiding the 'saviour complex' is crucial in these endeavors. It's about empowering those in need, providing them with the tools and opportunities to improve their situations. It's a partnership rather than a rescue mission, emphasizing respect, dignity, and mutual benefit.

For individuals wondering how they can contribute to building this culture, the answer lies in simple, everyday actions. Volunteer, donate, educate yourself and others, offer your skills and time, be kind to your neighbors, and share stories of kindness on your social media platforms. Every small act contributes to a larger movement.

At the heart of all charitable endeavors is the belief in collective human goodness and the power of compassion. Building a culture of kindness is an ambitious goal, but it is achievable. It requires persistent efforts, a shift in mindset, and the determination to make kindness a universal value.

Let's envision a future where our default is to care, to help, and to uplift. This isn't just an idealistic dream but a tangible goal that can start with a single act of kindness today. As we close this chapter on charity and look towards the future, we see a world brimming with potential for transformation. A world where kindness is the foundation upon which societies thrive.

In summary, building a culture of kindness is an endeavor that spans individual actions, education, storytelling, technology, corporate responsibility, and community involvement. It's about creating an environment where kindness is valued, celebrated, and multiplied. With each step we take in this direction, we pave the way for a more compassionate, empathetic, and charitable world.

As we move forward, let us carry with us the lessons learned, the stories shared, and the vision of a kinder world firmly within our hearts and minds. It's a journey that each of us can contribute to, a path that we can walk together. Let's step forward with kindness leading the way, transforming our communities, and, ultimately, our world one act of kindness at a time.

Chapter 13:
Advocacy and Activism:
Loud Voices for Quiet Needs

In the vibrant tapestry of charitable efforts, advocacy and activism stand out as powerful threads, weaving together the voices of those often left in the shadows. This chapter delves into the crucial role that advocacy plays in the realm of charity, shedding light on the silent battles fought every day for the underprivileged and overlooked. Raising awareness isn't just about speaking louder; it's about speaking smarter, ensuring that the right messages reach the right ears at the right time. The stories and strategies of successful campaigns for change reveal a common thread: passion paired with purpose can ignite a movement that traverses borders and breaks down barriers. From harnessing the power of social media to organizing grassroots movements, the landscape of activism is as diverse as it is dynamic.

But at its heart, advocacy is more than just campaigns and hashtags. It's about connecting on a human level, empathizing with the struggles of others, and using our voices to amplify theirs. Whether it's fighting for better healthcare, education, environmental protection, or human rights, activists around the globe remind us that change is always within our grasp if we're willing to reach for it. As we explore the intricate dance between advocacy and charity, we'll discover how even the quietest needs can be met with loud voices, calling for action, calling for compassion, and, most importantly, calling for change. In this journey, we'll learn that each of us holds the power to make a difference, not just in the lives of individuals, but in the fabric of society itself, stitching together a future where no need goes unheard and no hand goes unheld.

The Power of Raising Awareness

In the vast landscape of advocacy and activism, the ability to shed light on underrepresented issues stands as a testament to human empathy and solidarity. Raising awareness is not just about garnering attention; it's about educating the public, rallying support, and ultimately driving tangible changes that alleviate the struggles of those in need. Through strategic communication, compelling storytelling, and the relentless pursuit of justice, activists empower communities to not only recognize but also act upon social injustices that might otherwise go unnoticed. This tool of transformation creates a ripple effect, inspiring others to contribute their voice or resources, thereby multiplying the impact of charitable efforts. In essence, raising awareness transforms passive observers into active participants in the global mission to uplift and support those facing adversity. It's a vital step in a larger journey towards building a more compassionate and equitable world, where every individual is empowered to make a difference. By engaging in this critical endeavor, we not only highlight the silent struggles but also ignite a collective movement towards lasting change.

Successful Campaigns for Change In the realm of advocacy and activism, there have been countless initiatives aimed at fostering a better world — campaigns that not only appealed to the better angels of our nature but also achieved tangible results. These successful endeavors serve as a beacon, illuminating the path for future efforts in charitable works and social change.

Consider the environmental movement, which saw a significant victory with the establishment of Earth Day in 1970. A grassroots effort that galvanized millions across the globe, Earth Day's founding marked a turning point in public awareness about environmental issues. The campaign spurred action at all levels, leading to policy changes and the establishment of crucial environmental protections. It demonstrated that when people unite for a cause, they can alter the course of history.

Similarly, the civil rights movement in the United States during the 1960s proved the power of collective action for societal change. Through persistent activism, including marches, sit-ins, and legal challenges, the movement achieved monumental legal victories against racial segregation and discrimination. It showed that change, while often slow, is always possible with dedication and perseverance.

In recent years, the fight for marriage equality stands out as a stellar example of advocacy leading to change. A concerted effort by activists, legal experts, and everyday citizens transformed public opinion and, ultimately, the law. This campaign culminated in the historic 2015 Supreme Court ruling that legalized same-sex marriage nationwide, marking a significant stride toward equality.

Another impactful campaign is the global effort to combat HIV/AIDS. Starting in the late 20th century, activists worked tirelessly to destigmatize the disease, advocate for medical research, and secure funding for treatment and prevention. Their relentless efforts have significantly reduced HIV-related deaths and improved the quality of life for millions around the world.

The MeToo movement, initiated in 2006 but gaining global prominence in 2017, showcases the power of storytelling in advocacy. By encouraging survivors of sexual assault and harassment to share their experiences, the movement sparked a global conversation about consent, power dynamics, and institutional complicity in abuse. MeToo has led to policy changes, heightened awareness, and a shift in cultural attitudes regarding sexual misconduct.

On the front of educational reform, the campaign for universal primary education has made remarkable strides. Organizations like UNESCO have spearheaded initiatives that emphasize the importance of accessible education for all children, regardless of their circumstances. Through persistent advocacy and partnership with local governments, there have been significant increases in school enrollment rates in developing countries.

In the fight against poverty, the Make Poverty History campaign mobilized millions around the goal of eradicating extreme poverty. By advocating for fair trade, debt relief, and aid increases for the world's poorest countries, the campaign influenced agendas at major global summits and contributed to substantial policy changes and commitments from world leaders.

The water conservation movement, crucial in today's context of climate change and resource scarcity, has successfully campaigned for policies and practices that protect fresh water sources. Efforts by NGOs and community groups have led to innovative water management practices and increased public awareness about the importance of conserving water for future generations.

The campaign for animal rights has also seen significant victories, from the banning of cosmetic testing on animals in several countries to the closure of numerous fur farms and the adoption of stricter wildlife protection laws. These successes highlight society's growing recognition of the moral imperative to treat all living beings with respect and compassion.

In the sphere of public health, the anti-smoking campaigns of the past decades have produced dramatic shifts in public attitudes and behaviors towards tobacco use. Through a combination of education, legislation, and litigation, these campaigns have contributed to a significant decrease in smoking rates and related illnesses globally.

The push for mental health awareness has also gained momentum, with campaigns focused on destigmatizing mental illness and advocating for better access to treatment. By bringing personal stories into the public eye and lobbying for policy change, these efforts have begun to break down the barriers that prevent people from seeking help.

Climate change activism, epitomized by the School Strike for Climate initiative led by young activists around the world, has succeeded in thrusting the issue of global warming into the political and public consciousness. These campaigns have pressured governments and corporations to commit to more sustainable practices and policies.

The fight for gender equality has seen transformative campaigns that challenge systemic discrimination and violence against women. From grassroots organizing to influence global policy like the UN's Sustainable Development Goals, these campaigns are slowly but steadfastly making progress toward a more equitable world.

Each of these campaigns shares a common thread: a deep belief in the possibility of change. Through creativity, resilience, and the collective action of individuals united by a common cause, they have reshaped societies and touched the lives of millions. These stories of successful campaigns for change not only inspire but also teach us the invaluable lesson that when we come together, there's no limit to what we can achieve.

Chapter 14:
Legal and Ethical Aspects of Charity

In the realm of giving and aiding, while our hearts lead the charge, it's the framework of law and ethics that ensures our efforts reach their full potential without unintended consequences. Navigating the legalities of charitable work isn't just a matter of compliance; it's a fundamental expression of our commitment to do good in the world responsibly. As individuals driven to make a difference, understanding the corners of non-profit regulations and the ethical considerations in providing aid helps in crafting efforts that are not only impactful but also sustainable and respectful. It's about making sure that our desire to help doesn't inadvertently harm or infringe upon the dignity and autonomy of those we aim to assist.

Moreover, this chapter delves into the fabric that holds our best intentions and the mechanisms of law together, striking a delicate balance between passion and prudence. It's easy to be led by emotion in our quest to address inequities and sufferings, but a solid grasp of the ethical complexities and legal boundaries ensures that our help is meaningful and enduring. By equipping ourselves with this knowledge, we're not just adhering to rules; we're honoring the very essence of charity - to elevate, empower, and enrich lives without causing collateral damage. Ensuring that our actions are lawful and ethical is not just about mitigating risks; it's a profound expression of respect for the communities we serve and the cause we hold dear.

Understanding Non-Profit Regulations

In the heart of creating lasting and meaningful change through charity, lies the crucial understanding of the various rules and regulations that govern non-profit organizations. Just as the blueprint of a building ensures its stability and functionality, so too do the regulations for non-profits ensure their integrity, transparency, and the ethical use of resources. Grasping the legal framework isn't just about complying with the law; it's about scaffolding the trust between a charity and its supporters, making sure that every dollar donated turns into a stepping stone towards a better, more just world. It's about navigating the fine line between ambition and overreach, ensuring that the zeal to make a difference doesn't inadvertently lead down a path of non-compliance, which could tarnish the very cause one aims to elevate. In a landscape often painted with skepticism, understanding and adhering to these regulations is a beacon of credibility, inviting more hands to join in the effort. Whether you're at the helm of a charity or looking to contribute to a cause, a solid foundation in non-profit regulations not only enriches your endeavor but steels it against the inevitable challenges that come with chasing a vision larger than life.

Navigating the Complexities of Aid Navigating through the intricacies of providing aid is akin to threading a needle in the intricate fabric of global humanitarian efforts. As we delve into this sub-section, it's essential to understand that offering help isn't always as straightforward as it may seem. The path to effective assistance is paved with challenges, regulations, and ethical dilemmas.

The ethos behind charity and offering aid is undeniably noble. Yet, beneath the surface, lies a complex web of considerations that must be navigated with care, empathy, and a deep understanding of the broader impact. The first step is recognizing that while the impulse to help is universal, the execution requires meticulous planning and awareness of local contexts.

In recent times, the call for aid has become louder and more urgent, with crises emerging around the globe at an alarming rate. But as we respond to these calls, it's crucial to identify the right form of help. Not all aid is equal, and what works in one context may not in another. It demands a thoughtful approach that respects the recipient's dignity and autonomy.

One significant challenge is overcoming the 'saviour complex' — the belief that one has the absolute solution to another's problem. This complex can overshadow the needs and desires of those being helped, denying them a voice in their own recovery process. Therefore, engaging with communities to understand their needs and involving them in solution development is vital.

Furthermore, the sustainability of aid is a pressing concern. Providing support that offers short-term relief but fails to create long-term sustainability can do more harm than good. As such, the focus should shift to building resilience and empowering communities to become self-reliant over time.

The implementation of aid is subject to various laws and regulations, both domestic and international. These are designed to protect both donors and recipients but can also pose barriers to timely and effective assistance. Navigating these legal frameworks requires knowledge and patience, ensuring that aid efforts are compliant yet impactful.

Ethical considerations are at the heart of providing aid. Questions of fairness, equity, and justice cannot be overlooked. It is not enough to provide aid; it must be done in a way that respects the rights and dignity of those receiving it. This ethical compass should guide every decision made in the aid process.

In the era of global connectivity, technology has become a critical tool in navigating the complexities of aid. Digital platforms can enhance transparency, accountability, and efficiency in aid delivery. However, they also raise concerns about data protection, privacy, and the digital divide. Harnessing technology responsibly can be a game-changer in the field of humanitarian assistance.

Collaboration and partnership stand out as fundamental elements in overcoming aid challenges. No single entity can address the multifaceted nature of humanitarian crises alone. By working together, organizations can pool resources, share expertise, and amplify their impact.

The measure of success in navigating aid complexities is not just in the amount of help provided but in the quality and sustainability of that assistance. The true victory lies in leaving communities stronger, more resilient, and better equipped to face future challenges.

Monitoring and evaluation play critical roles in this realm. They allow for the assessment of aid effectiveness, providing valuable feedback that can inform future efforts. This cycle of learning and improvement is crucial for the evolution of aid strategies and the maximization of their impact.

Transparency and accountability are non-negotiable in the world of aid. They foster trust between donors, implementing organizations, and the communities they serve. Building this trust requires a clear and honest communication about intentions, actions, and outcomes.

Finally, the emotional and psychological aspects of offering and receiving aid must not be underestimated. The process can be fraught with frustration, disappointment, but also hope and joy. Recognizing the human element in this complex equation is essential for maintaining empathy and compassion in our efforts to help.

As we navigate the complexities of aid, it is this blend of practical wisdom, ethical commitment, and emotional intelligence that will guide us through. The journey is challenging, fraught with obstacles and heartbreak, but it is also immensely rewarding. The opportunity to make a tangible difference in the lives of those in need is a privilege that comes with great responsibility.

In conclusion, understanding the multifaceted nature of aid is critical to its success. As we strive to offer a helping hand, let us do so with mindfulness, humility, and a steadfast commitment to empowering those we seek to help. This journey, though complex, is a testament to our shared humanity and the indomitable spirit of compassion that unites us all.

Chapter 15:
Measuring Impact:
The Real Success of Charity

In the journey of philanthropy, where hearts are touched and lives are transformed, the penultimate measure of achievement isn't found merely in the magnitudes of contributions but in the depths of impacts made. *Measuring Impact: The Real Success of Charity* shifts the gaze from the quantifiable to the qualitative, from the exhaustive tallies of donations to the intimate narratives of change. It's one thing to know how many dollars were spent or how many goods were distributed, but quite another, and more profound, to grasp how those resources altered individual destinies and uplifted communities. The true essence of charity resonates not in the echo of resources spent but in the silent, yet powerful, waves of transformation that ripple through societies, revolutionizing lives in their wake.

Understanding the real success of charity calls for a redefined lens, one that sees beyond the numbers and recognizes the stories behind the statistics. These stories of transformation—of despair turned into hope, of scarcity turned into abundance—paint a vivid picture of what it genuinely means to make a difference. It challenges us to question our impact, to look at the faces behind the figures, and to evaluate our efforts not just by the input, but by the outcome. As we delve into this chapter, we're invited to reflect on the holistic effectiveness of our charitable actions, pushing us to consider how we, as individuals and communities, can foster a legacy of meaningful change that transcends time and numbers. The real success of charity, therefore, isn't just about how much we give, but how well we give, ensuring that each act of kindness truly counts in the grand canvas of human solidarity.

Beyond the Numbers

In our journey to assess the real success of charity, it's crucial to recognize that seldom can the full scope of impact be captured by mere statistics or percentages. True success lies in the shimmer of hope reignited in someone's eyes, in the restored dignity to those who had none, and in the empowerment of communities to stand on their own. These are the stories that don't just resonate on paper but echo in the hearts of those affected and inspire others to partake in this chain reaction of kindness. By focusing solely on quantitative evaluation, one might overlook the profound personal and societal transformations charity begets—transformations where empathy transcends boundaries, and collective action paves the way for a future where assistance isn't an exception but a norm. As such, diving 'Beyond the Numbers' allows us to appreciate the intricate tapestry of change woven by acts of charity, where every thread represents a life touched, a despair mitigated, and a new chapter written in the saga of human solidarity.

Stories of Transformation Each tale begins not with a grand gesture, but with a simple act of kindness, a spark that ignites the potent possibility of change. These stories are not just narratives; they are testaments to the profound impacts that charity can have on the lives of individuals and communities worldwide. The essence of giving transcends borders, cultures, and socio-economic statuses, proving that at the heart of kindness, lies the power to transform.

In a remote village where access to clean water was a luxury, a single well funded by a small charity reshaped the future of the entire community. Children who once spent hours each day fetching water from distant sources now had time to attend school. Women, released from the perpetual task of water collection, began small businesses, revolutionizing their roles within the village. This story illustrates that charity's impact often extends beyond its initial intent, fostering opportunities for education and economic empowerment.

On the streets of a bustling city, a homeless man, once a gifted teacher, found a new beginning when a passerby decided to listen to his story. This chance encounter led to a crowdfunding campaign that not only restored the man's dignity but also reinstated him into a profession where he could once again nurture young minds. This narrative underscores the notion that sometimes, a helping hand can reopen doors that seemed forever closed.

In a different setting, a rural health clinic operated on the verge of closure received a lifeline from charity donations that not only kept its doors open but also upgraded its facilities. The clinic's transformation meant that maternal mortality in the region plummeted, illustrating how strategic charitable actions can address critical health challenges, saving lives, and safeguarding futures.

Then there were the efforts of a youth organization that transformed a derelict city lot into a vibrant community garden. This initiative not only beautified the neighborhood but also fostered a sense of community ownership and responsibility. It demonstrated how charity, when channeled through communal efforts, can cultivate more than just crops—it can grow resilience, pride, and a shared purpose among neighbors.

In the world of education, a scholarship funded by charitable giving became the key for a bright but underprivileged student to unlock her potential. Her journey from a cramped, one-room house to graduating top of her class was a powerful reminder of how charity can light the way for extraordinary talent to emerge from the most unlikely places.

There's a story of environmental charity, where a campaign to save an endangered species led not only to its recovery but also to the revitalization of an entire ecosystem. This achievement illustrated the ripple effect of charity, showing how saving one piece of the natural puzzle can benefit a whole ecosystem, promoting biodiversity and sustainability.

In the aftermath of natural disasters, stories abound of communities rebuilt and lives restored through charitable efforts. One striking account involved a small fishing village that, after being decimated by a tsunami, was restored not just in infrastructure but in spirit, thanks to the global outpouring of support. This tale exemplifies the collective power of charity to heal and rebuild in the face of devastating loss.

The process of transformation is often marked by small victories, as seen in a literacy program that started with a few books in a makeshift classroom. Over time, this program blossomed into a full-fledged library, igniting a passion for reading and learning in a community where illiteracy had once seemed insurmountable. This shift highlighted how incremental contributions can lead to monumental outcomes in education.

On an individual level, a young man's life was radically altered when a charitable organization provided him with a prosthetic limb. Freed from the constraints of his disability, he became not just mobile but an advocate for the disabled, using his story to inspire and drive change. His journey is a testament to the individual empowerment that can flow from charitable acts.

In an urban neighborhood plagued by youth violence, a charity-initiated mentorship program helped redirect the lives of many at-risk teens towards constructive activities and education. Years later, some of these teens returned as mentors themselves, proving how charity can break cycles of negativity and create cycles of positivity and growth instead.

The effectiveness of charity is not confined to its immediate recipients. In one story, a family that received aid during a time of crisis later founded a charity to support others in similar situations. Their transformation from beneficiaries to benefactors is a compelling example of how the act of receiving charity can instill a lasting commitment to giving.

A tale from the tech world involves a charitable initiative that provided laptops to underprivileged children, enabling them to access online education and compete on equal footing with their peers. This narrative highlighted the democratizing power of charitable giving in the digital age, removing barriers and leveling the playing field for all.

In conclusion, these stories of transformation serve as unequivocal evidence of the deep and varied impacts of charity. They remind us that behind every act of giving lies the potential for a profound change, encouraging us to look beyond the immediate act to the ripples of hope and opportunity that follow. Let these narratives inspire us to extend our hands in charity, for in doing so, we play a part in shaping a kinder, more equitable world.

Conclusion

In the span of the pages we've traversed together, we've embarked on a journey deep into the heart of what charity truly means. From its humble beginnings etched in the annals of history to its vibrant, unstoppable force in modern society, charity emerged as an undeniable testament to the capacity of human kindness. This journey, though varied and intricate, brings us to a singular, inescapable conclusion: the act of giving, in its purest form, is among the most profound expressions of our shared humanity.

Reflecting on the global view of charity, we've seen that despite our diverse cultures and backgrounds, the intention to help those in need bridges the divide, creating a universal language understood by all. It deepens our connection to one another, reminding us that, at our core, we're not all that different. The fabric of charity, woven with threads of empathy and compassion, blankets the world, offering warmth to those in the shadows of hardship.

As we delved into the psychological benefits of being charitable, it became clear that the act of giving extends beyond mere altruism. It's a pathway to personal fulfillment, a means through which we find joy, purpose, and even healing. Helping others isn't just about making a difference in their lives; it's about transforming our own, experiencing the unparalleled satisfaction that comes from knowing we've contributed to something larger than ourselves.

The narratives of personal stories we've encountered—tales of hope, help, and the incredible resilience of the human spirit—stand as powerful testaments to charity's impact. These stories don't just inform; they inspire, urging us to take action, to be the change we wish to see. Each story carries a reminder that we all have something valuable to offer, be it time, resources, or a listening ear.

Addressing the challenges of charity provoked thoughtful consideration of our responsibilities. It urged us to approach our charitable endeavors with humility, ensuring our efforts are sustainable and respectful, always prioritizing the dignity and autonomy of those we aim to assist. We were prompted to look beyond good intentions, striving for actions that truly empower and uplift.

The intersection of technology and charity illuminated fascinating evolutions in how we give. With the world more connected than ever, we've uncovered new opportunities to reach those in need, transcending geographical barriers to create global communities of support. This digital frontier invites us to innovate, to leverage the tools at our disposal to make giving more accessible and impactful.

Our exploration of corporate social responsibility showcased the power of ethical business practices. When companies act as stewards of the community, seeing beyond profit to their role in society, they set a precedent for what it means to give back. This relationship between commerce and charity highlights the potential for a more compassionnate marketplace, where success is measured not just by revenue, but by contribution to the common good.

Confronting the dark side of charity was a necessary journey into the complexities of aid. It was a stark reminder that our actions, however well-intentioned, must be guided by vigilance and a commitment to ensuring that our contributions do indeed count. In doing so, we safeguard the integrity of charitable work, ensuring that help reaches those who need it most, free from exploitation or misuse.

Volunteerism emerged as the backbone of charitable endeavors, a vigorous affirmation of what individuals can achieve when driven by a collective purpose. The commitment of volunteers—those tireless guardians of goodwill—serves as a beacon, encouraging us all to find our own ways to contribute, to discover the profound satisfaction that comes from lending our strength to a cause greater than ourselves.

Looking ahead, the future of charity holds limitless potential. Innovations in giving promise new horizons of assistance and support, inviting us to imagine a world where charity is integrated into the very fabric of society. As we build this future together, our actions today lay the groundwork for a culture of kindness, where the impulse to help is a universal characteristic of the human experience.

Advocacy and activism have shown us that voices raised in unison can achieve monumental change. By advocating for those in the margins, we reaffirm our commitment to a just and equable world, where everyone has the opportunity to thrive. These loud voices for quiet needs remind us of the power we hold when we stand together, united by compassion and the resolve to make a difference.

Through the lens of legal and ethical aspects, we were reminded of the importance of navigating charity with awareness and response-bility. Understanding the framework that governs charitable actions ensures that our endeavors are not only effective but also adhere to principles of integrity and transparency.

Measuring the impact of charity transcends numbers and statistics; it's found in the stories of lives transformed, communities rebuilt, and hope rekindled. These stories, as diverse as they are poignant, underscore the true success of charity—not just in what is given, but in what is gained: strength, solidarity, and a shared belief in the promise of a better tomorrow.

In conclusion, our exploration of charity has been a journey of understanding, reflection, and, most importantly, inspiration. As we turn the final page of this chapter, let the lessons contained within not simply linger as thoughts but propel us into action. Let us move forward with the conviction that each act of kindness, no matter how small, is a step towards a more compassionate world. In the spirit of charity, let us extend our hands, open our hearts, and embrace the boundless potential of human generosity. Together, we have the power to make a difference—one act of kindness at a time.

Appendix A:
Appendix

As we draw the curtains on our journey through the realms of charity, understanding its essence, navigating its challenges, and looking toward its future, it's crucial to recognize that this is not the end. Far from it, this is a beginning—a call to action for each of us to make generosity and assistance central themes in our lives. Within these pages, we've explored charity's multifaceted nature, its universal value beyond religious confines, and its profound ability to transform both the giver and the receiver. Now, it's time to translate knowledge into action.

Resources for Getting Involved

One of the first steps toward actualizing the spirit of charity is knowing where to start. Many of us yearn to make a difference but find ourselves overwhelmed by the sheer number of causes and organizations out there. To harness that goodwill effectively, we've compiled a curated list of resources designed to connect you with opportunities that align with your interests, abilities, and the needs of the community.

VolunteerMatch.org: A platform that connects volunteers with non-profit organizations in need of assistance. Whether your passion lies in environmental conservation, education, or healthcare, there's a place for you.

Charity Navigator: Before you donate your hard-earned money, ensure it's going to make a real impact. Charity Navigator evaluates charities based on their transparency, financial health, and accountability to help you make informed choices.

GiveWell: For those who want to ensure their donations go towards the most effective causes, GiveWell conducts in-depth research to recommend charities where donations can save or improve lives the most.

Further Reading

To deepen your understanding of charity and continue to be inspired, further reading is invaluable. Knowledge is not just power; it's also motivation, guidance, and illumination. Here are a few recommendations that can expand your horizon and possibly change the way you view giving and sharing in this interconnected world.

The Life You Can Save by Peter Singer: A compelling argument for why we should be doing more to improve the lives of people living in extreme poverty around the globe.

Give and Take by Adam Grant: This book explores how our interactions with others can lead to success, and why giving often leads to receiving in the world of business and beyond.

Doing Good Better by William MacAskill: MacAskill introduces the concept of effective altruism and offers practical advice for making a significant impact through our charitable actions.

In the final analysis, charity is about much more than just providing aid; it's about building connections, fostering empathy, and creating a world where compassion compels action. As you reflect on the insights and stories woven through this book, let them be more than just narratives and data. Let them be a spark that ignites a lifelong commitment to making a difference, no matter how big or small.

Remember, in the tapestry of humanity, every thread counts. Your contribution, your step toward helping others, weaves into the larger picture a brighter, kinder future for all.

Resources for Getting Involved

The journey into the heart of charity and giving back isn't just a path walked alone; it's a road built on the foundation of community, shared purpose, and mutual aid. In this expansive section, we're diving into an arsenal of resources aimed at equipping you with the tools, knowledge, and connections to make a tangible impact in the world of charity. Whether you're new to charitable endeavors or looking to deepen your existing commitments, there's something here for everyone.

First and foremost, understanding the vast landscape of charity requires navigating through a plethora of organizations, causes, and missions. A good starting point is to identify your passion. Ask yourself what issues resonate deeply with you. Is it eliminating hunger, providing education to the underprivileged, or fighting climate change? Once you've pinpointed your passion, the next steps become clearer.

There's an incredible array of databases and directories online that list non-profits and charities by category, mission, and location. Sites like GuideStar and Charity Navigator are invaluable tools for researching potential organizations to support. They provide detailed information including mission statements, impact evidence, financial health, and transparency. This research is crucial, as it ensures your time, energy, and resources contribute to causes with proven track records of making a difference.

Volunteering your time is one of the most direct ways to get involved. Platforms like VolunteerMatch or Idealist can connect you with local and global opportunities tailored to your skills and interests. Whether it's helping with local food drives, tutoring students online, or collaborating with a global health initiative, every action contributes to a larger chain of kindness and impact.

For those drawn to the innovation that technology brings to charity, exploring crowdfunding platforms like GoFundMe or Kickstarter's socially-focused campaigns can be incredibly rewarding. These platforms allow individuals and organizations to raise funds for causes, projects, and people in need, democratizing the process of charitable giving and allowing anyone with an internet connection to contribute to meaningful change.

Corporate social responsibility (CSR) is another avenue through which one can engage in charity. If you're part of an organization, advocating for your workplace to adopt socially responsible practices, support charitable causes, or match employee donations can amplify the impact of your charitable efforts. Many companies are already recognizing the importance of giving back and are keen to support initiatives brought forward by their employees.

Yet, charity isn't only about donating money or time; it's also about using your voice. Advocacy and activism play critical roles in bringing about systemic changes. Educating yourself on the issues, signing petitions, attending community meetings, and using social media to raise awareness are all forms of involvement that can spearhead change. In this digital age, the power of a shared story or a social media campaign to rally support for a cause cannot be underestimated.

For those interested in volunteerism, it's essential to recognize that the benefits extend both ways. Not only do your efforts contribute positively to the community, but volunteering can also provide you with valuable skills, experiences, and connections. Reflect on what you hope to gain from your volunteer experience, such as leadership skills, a deeper understanding of a particular issue, or the chance to meet like-minded individuals. This reflection can guide you towards opportunities that align with your personal and professional growth objectives.

In the realm of legal and ethical considerations, it's crucial for anyone looking to dive deep into charity work to familiarize themselves with the regulations and ethical guidelines that govern non-profit organizations and charitable giving. Resources such as the Council on Foundations or the National Council of Nonprofits offer guides, webinars, and workshops to educate donors and volunteers on these important topics, ensuring your efforts are effective, ethical, and compliant.

Measuring the impact of your charitable efforts is another fundamental aspect of getting involved. Understanding how to assess the effectiveness of a charity or a specific initiative can guide your decisions and help you identify the most impactful ways to contribute. This involves looking at measurable outcomes, personal stories of transformation, and the transparency of the organization in question.

Building a community around your charitable efforts can amplify your impact and provide support, motivation, and camaraderie along the journey. Engage with local community centers, online forums, or social media groups focused on charity and volunteerism. Sharing experiences, advice, and encouragement in these spaces can be incredibly enriching.

Lastly, it's important to remember that the journey of giving back is a personal one. It can be easy to compare your contributions to others, but charity is not a competition. Whether you choose to volunteer your time locally, donate to global causes, or advocate for change within your community, your efforts make a difference. Celebrate the steps you're taking and know that every act of kindness contributes to a larger wave of positive change.

In conclusion, the resources for getting involved in charity are as diverse as they are plentiful. From leveraging technology and platforms that connect volunteers with causes, to engaging in advocacy and raising awareness, the paths to contributing to a better world are manifold. Remember, the most crucial step is the first one: deciding to make a difference. Armed with the resources and insights shared here, you're well-equipped to embark on a fulfilling journey of charity and giving back.

As you move forward, carry with you the understanding that charity is a deeply human undertaking. It's about forging connections, understanding needs, and responding with empathy and action. With each step, you're not just giving back; you're also growing, learning, and becoming part of a global community of people committed to making the world a better place. Let this guide be your starting point, and let your heart and your actions lead the way.

Embracing charity in its many forms is a testament to our shared humanity and compassion. It is through our collective efforts that we can confront challenges, lift each other up, and foster a future marked by generosity and kindness. As you venture into the world of giving, do so with an open heart, a curious mind, and the unwavering belief that your contributions, no matter the size, have the power to effect real, lasting change.

Further Reading

In the journey toward fostering a deeper understanding of charity and the profound impact it has on both givers and receivers, further reading serves not just as an expansion of knowledge, but as a beacon that guides us toward the ways we can offer a helping hand when necessary. This section aims to equip you with a curated list of publications that delve into various aspects of charity, philanthropy, volunteerism, and the essence of human kindness. Whether you are seeking to deepen your understanding, find inspiration, or explore the practical aspects of contributing to a cause, these texts offer valuable insights.

The concept of charity, while universally understood, is richly layered and complex. It emanates from various motivations and takes on multiple forms across different cultures and societies. To begin unraveling this complexity, "The Altruistic Imagination: A History of Social Work and Social Policy in the United States" by John H. Ehrenreich provides an in-depth historical viewpoint on how charity and social work have evolved in the context of U.S. society and policy. It lays a foundation for understanding the roots of organized charity and its progression into the modern era.

Understanding the psychological underpinnings of why we give is another compelling aspect of charity. "The Giving Way to Happiness: Stories and Science Behind the Transformative Power of Giving" by Jenny Santi taps into the joy and fulfillment derived from giving. Through a mix of poignant stories and scientific evidence, this book illustrates how acts of kindness can improve our mental and emotional well-being.

To grasp the global perspective on charity, "Doing Good Better: How Effective Altruism Can Help You Make a Difference" by William MacAskill explores the concept of effective altruism, focusing on how we can use our resources most effectively to help others. It challenges traditional notions of charity and proposes a more analytical approach to doing good, making it a thought-provoking read for anyone interested in maximizing their impact.

Charity within the family context is another area ripe for exploration. "Raising Charitable Children" by Carol Weisman offers practical advice and strategies for parents eager to instill the values of generosity and empathy in their children. It highlights the significance of charity beginning at home and provides a blueprint for nurturing a spirit of giving in the next generation.

The digital realm has transformed how we engage with charitable causes. "The Digital Transformation of Social Work: Technology for Inclusion, Advocacy, and Social Change" edited by Lauri Goldkind, Lea Wolf, and Paul P. Freddolino delves into how technology is reshaping the landscape of giving and volunteerism, highlighting both the opportunities and challenges presented by this shift.

Corporate social responsibility (CSR) represents another facet of the modern approach to charity. "Corporate Social Responsibility: Doing the Most Good for Your Company and Your Cause" by Philip Kotler and Nancy Lee offers insights into how businesses can effectively integrate social good into their operational model, shedding light on the intersection between profit and purpose.

However, navigating the complexities and pitfalls of charity requires caution and wisdom. "Toxic Charity: How Churches and Charities Hurt Those They Help (And How to Reverse It)" by Robert D. Lupton provides a critical examination of how well-intentioned aid can sometimes do more harm than good. It offers valuable lessons on ensuring that help is both respectful and empowering.

Volunteerism acts as the backbone of many charitable endeavors, and understanding the multifaceted nature of volunteering can enhance one's contributions significantly. "The Volunteer Management Handbook: Leadership Strategies for Success" edited by Tracy D. Connors is a comprehensive guide that covers various aspects of volunteer engagement and management, making it an essential resource for anyone involved in organizing or participating in volunteer activities.

Looking toward the future, "The Life You Can Save: Acting Now to End World Poverty" by Peter Singer challenges readers to consider the role of personal responsibility in addressing global poverty. It discusses innovative ways of giving and acts as a call to action for making philanthropy a fundamental part of our lives.

Advocacy and activism represent vital aspects of the charitable sphere, and "A Path Appears: Transforming Lives, Creating Opportunity" by Nicholas D. Kristof and Sheryl WuDunn showcases remarkable stories of how individuals and organizations are using their voices and resources to fight for social justice and improve lives. It serves as an inspirational reminder of the power each person has to make a difference.

Understanding the legal and ethical considerations of charity is crucial for ensuring that efforts are not only heartfelt but also effective and transparent. "Charity Law & Social Policy: National and International Perspectives on the Functions of the Law Relating to Charities" by Kerry O'Halloran provides an in-depth examination of the regulatory environment surrounding charitable organizations and their operations, offering readers insight into the importance of governance and accountability in the nonprofit sector.

Lastly, measuring the true success of charitable efforts goes beyond mere numbers. "The Science of Giving: Experimental Approaches to the Study of Charity" edited by Daniel M. Oppenheimer and Christopher Y. Olivola brings together research from psychology, economics, marketing, and philanthropy to explore how and why people decide to give to charity. It provides a data-driven look at what makes charitable endeavors successful, enriched with insights that can inform both personal and organizational giving strategies.

As you explore these further readings, may you find not just information, but inspiration. May the pages of these books expand your understanding, challenge your perceptions, and most importantly, inspire you to act. The need for a helping hand and a kind heart is ever-present in our world, and through continued learning, we can all find new ways to contribute to a culture of kindness and generosity.

In conclusion, these texts serve not merely as an academic exercise but as a call to action. They remind us of the beauty of human compassion and the incredible impact that charity can have on both the giver and the receiver. As we move forward, let us carry with us the lessons learned and the stories shared, forging a path toward a future where charity in all its forms is celebrated and cultivated.